FOODS *of the* AMERICAS

≈ Northern Shoshone woman winnowing grain, 1904.
Lemhi Reservation, Idaho. (N22367)

ESSAYS BY

George P. Horse Capture (A'aninin)

Millie Knapp (Anishinabe/Tuscarora)

Marty Kreipe de Montaño (Prairie Band Potawatomi)

Marcus Monenerkit (Comanche)

Nicolasa I. Sandoval (Chumash)

Susan Secakuku (Hopi)

Thomas W. Sweeney (Citizen Potawatomi)

Karenne Wood (Monacan)

Elizabeth Woody (Navajo/Warm Springs/Wasco/Yakama)

FOOD PHOTOGRAPHY BY

Maren Caruso

FOODS *of the* AMERICAS

NATIVE RECIPES AND TRADITIONS

Fernando and Marlene Divina

TEN SPEED PRESS
Berkeley | Toronto

in association with

SMITHSONIAN NATIONAL MUSEUM OF THE AMERICAN INDIAN

≋ DEDICATED TO CLARA ROSE LATRAY NORDBERG ≋

(TURTLE MOUNTAIN BAND OF CHIPPEWA)

Ten Speed Press
Box 7123
Berkeley, California 94707
www.tenspeed.com

Distributed in Australia by Simon and Schuster Australia, in
Canada by Ten Speed Press Canada, in New Zealand by South-
ern Publishers Group, in South Africa by Real Books, and in the
United Kingdom and Europe by Airlift Book Company.

Cover and text design: Nancy Austin
Food and prop styling: Erin Quon and Kim Konecny
Food photographer's assistant: Faiza Ali

NMAI Head of Publications: Terence Winch
NMAI editors: Linda Martin and Sally Barrows

Printed in China
First printing, 2004

1 2 3 4 5 6 7 8 9 10 — 09 08 07 06 05 04

The Smithsonian National Museum of the American Indian
is dedicated to working in collaboration with the indigenous
peoples of the Americas to preserve, study, and exhibit the
life, languages, literature, history, and arts of the Native
peoples of the Western Hemisphere.

The museum's flagship building on the National Mall in
Washington, D.C., which opened in September 2004, prom-
ises to be one of the leading cultural destinations in the
world. The George Gustav Heye Center is one of New York
City's premier museums. The Cultural Resources Center in
Suitland, Maryland, houses the museum's collection and
serves as a research and conservation facility.

For information about the National Museum of the American Indian, visit www.AmericanIndian.si.edu. For information
about becoming a member, call (800) 242-6624.

Library of Congress Cataloging-in-Publication Data

Divina, Fernando.

Foods of the Americas : native recipes and traditions / Fernando
and Marlene Divina ; with essays by George P. Horse Capture . . .
[et al.].

p. cm.

"Published in association with the Smithsonian National Museum
of the American Indian."

Includes bibliographical references and index.

ISBN 1-58008-259-9 (hardcover)

1. Indian cookery. 2. Indians of North America—Food. I. Divina,
Marlene. II. Horse Capture, George P. III. National Museum of the
American Indian (U.S.). IV. Title.

TX715.D5883 2004

641.59'297—dc22   2004005792

Contents

Acknowledgments

We hope that *Foods of the Americas* will help celebrate and advance the food traditions of the Western Hemisphere's first inhabitants. We are forever in debt to all cooks who have preceded us and look forward to a new era in the evolution of American cuisine.

Without the generous support of family, friends, and colleagues, this book would not have come to be. First we thank the National Museum of the American Indian (NMAI) and Ten Speed Press for sharing our dream of seeing this book to fruition. We extend our gratitude to members of the design team of the NMAI, namely Duane Blue Spruce (Laguna and San Juan Pueblo), NMAI facilities planning coordinator; Johnpaul Jones (Cherokee/Choctaw); Kevin Carl of Jones & Jones Architects and Landscape Architects, Ltd.; ethnobotanist Donna House (Navajo/Oneida); and design consultant Ramona Sakiestewa (Hopi).

We are deeply appreciative of our editors, Amy Pastan, Linda R. Martin (Navajo), and Sally Barrows at NMAI and Holly Taines White at Ten Speed Press, for their precision and grammatical exactitude, and for keeping us centered. Our gratitude also goes to Terence Winch, Head of Publications at NMAI, who led in the development of the book; Ann Kawasaki of the Publications Department; and Lou Stancari of NMAI's Photo Services Department.

Diana Kennedy, along with her friend and fellow cookbook author Marilyn Tausend, has for years inspired and provided us with guidance and vivid instruction. Ethnobotanist and author E. Barrie Kavasch (Chickamauga Cherokee/Creek/Powhatan) shared her knowledge of Eastern Woodlands tribes and provided authoritative comment on others. Several renowned Native artists also contributed to the cultural flavor of the book: ceramist, sculptor, and elder Lillian Pitt (Yakama/Wasco/Warm Springs) opened a window to the world of the Columbia River Indians of the Northwest, while sculptor/printmaker Marvin Oliver (Quinault/Isleta Pueblo) and bead artist Marcus Amerman (Choctaw) inspired us with their stories as they taste-tested our recipes amidst their incredible artwork.

Thanks to the staff of the Billie Jane Baguley Library and Archives at the Heard Museum in Phoenix, Arizona. Special thanks to Jerry Anne Di Vecchio, food writer and a former senior editor of *Sunset* magazine, who gave us early guidance and support. Those who shared our vision and enthusiasm with industry peers include Sur la Table, the Blue Ribbon Cooking School, David Sarasohn, Karen Brooks, Carol Mighton Haddix, Nancy Freeman, Bridgette Oliver, Arnold Ball, Horst Mager, F. Robert Williamson, Sinclair Philip, Ron Zimmerman, Carrie van Dyke, Jerry Traunfeld, Tamara Murphy, Gayle Jolley, Fred and Amelia Hard, Barbara Durbin, Ginger Johnston, Eileen Bailey, Angela Allen, Nikki Buchanan, and Elin Jeffords.

Thanks to ecologist and ethnobotanist Dr. Gary Paul Nabhan for his critical role in the conservation and collection of Native seeds and preserving Native agricultural traditions in North America, particularly the Southwest. Thanks to Chinook jargon linguist Tony Johnson (Willapa), the community at Wyoming's Wind River Reservation, and to the Oregon-based anthropologist Melissa Darby for her instruction on a Northwest method of wapato harvesting.

Immediate and resounding support also came from the non-Native food industry experts, writers, and cooks—Deborah Madison, Barbara Pool Fenzl, Graham Kerr, Andre Soltner, Alice Waters, Jeremiah Tower, and Elizabeth Schneider—who have helped us along our path and support the concept of advancing indigenous foods through American cuisine.

To our relations, we extend a sincere thanks to the Divina, Nordberg, and Jennings families, including Melvin Ingvar Nordberg, Zona Jennings, John Wilson, Bob and Mary Parsons, Jonetta Nordberg Walter, Betty Sinclair and Richard Didzun, Janine Wolf, Sally Ervin, Kay Uhl, Karen Gilmore, Dennis and Cheryl Denton, the Denton family, Donald Crews, Ann Jonas, David Colley, Jason E. Merrill, Barb and Brian Williamson, and Fred and Jennifer Unger—for taste-testing with graciousness. To all of our staff, friends, and family, who endured our distractions to commit entirely to this book, we extend our deepest appreciation.

Posthumously, our heartfelt thanks to food writer Jonathan Suskind, and to Fernando's parents, Fernando Sr. and Wanda Divina.

Last, and most importantly, we thank our son, Zoey Xavier Divina. Without his altruistic support of this book and all of our endeavors we could not have succeeded.

FOREWORD: Native Taste

"On Thanksgiving Day, North Americans sometimes remember the Indians who gave them their cuisine by dining on turkey with cornbread stuffing, cranberry sauce, succotash, corn on the cob, sweet potato casserole, stewed squash and tomatoes, baked beans with maple syrup, and pecan pie. Few cooks or gourmets, however, recognize the much broader extent to which American Indian cuisine radically changed cooking and dining in every part of the globe, from Timbuktu to Tibet. Sichuan beef with chiles, German chocolate cake, curried potatoes, vanilla ice cream, Hungarian goulash, peanut brittle, and pizza all owe their primary flavorings to the American Indians."

—Jack Weatherford, *Indian Givers: How the Indians of the Americas Transformed the World*

Food keeps us alive, as we all know. Nourishment allows us to grow and be healthy. But good cooking takes us beyond survival and into the realms of culture and pleasure. In *Foods of the Americas* you will get a taste of the Native world and a sampling of Indian life and culture—for much can be known of a people by what they eat, how they prepare their meals, and what attitudes they bring to the table.

A community's food traditions are often a crucial element of that group's identity. Traditional food and food preparation are integral to many Native ceremonies and social gatherings, such as Pueblo Feast Days in the Southwest or potlatches in the Northwest. For the Maya, corn is the most important food, and all parts of the plant are considered sacred. For Northwest Coast peoples, salmon assume cultural centrality. It is no surprise to find important foods not only in a community's diet, but in its stories and histories as well. Throughout the indigenous world, food sources and traditions have strong spiritual connotations.

Many of these traditions are at the heart of this book, and a good book, like a good meal, requires all the right ingredients. In *Foods of the Americas*, I think you'll find that the authors, editors, and designer have collaborated to concoct an enticing volume. First off, I must thank the book's primary authors, Fernando and Marlene Divina, expert restaurateurs who have brought years of imaginative and practical experience with Native ingredients and traditions to bear upon the creation of the many wonderful recipes you will find herein. The recipes make very clear that the Native palate is impressively sophisticated. If you have the opportunity to visit the Mitsitam Café at our museum on the National Mall, you will be able to further sample the influence of the Divinas, who helped plan a menu that redefines the possibilities of museum restaurants.

This book, I am happy to report, gives us even more than the promise of many tasty future meals. Thanks to a stellar lineup of Native writers, many of them colleagues, we are able to offer readers something beyond the typical cookbook menu. Through their brief, lucid essays, we are given an insider's perspective on Native attitudes toward food and, by extension, to Indian life. I know you will gain a new appreciation of the traditional reservation foods of the northern Plains when you read the piece by my friend and colleague George P. Horse Capture (A'aninin), one of NMAI's most respected Native voices. Likewise, the essays by Millie Knapp (Anishinabe/Tuscarora), Marty Kreipe de Montaño (Prairie Band Potawatomi), Marcus Monenerkit (Comanche), Niki Sandoval (Chumash), Susan Secakuku (Hopi), Thomas Sweeney (Citizen Potawatomi), Karenne Wood (Monacan), and Elizabeth Woody (Navajo/Warm Springs/ Wasco/Yakama) all bring to life the vivid relationship between Indian people and the foods that sustain us.

I also extend our collective gratitude to former Smithsonian colleague Amy Pastan, who helped pull much of the initial material for the book together, and to NMAI editors Linda Martin (Navajo) and Sally Barrows, who worked hard to hammer out a variety of dents in the text. Also thanks to Terence Winch, head of our publications office, for directing the project; to Duane Blue Spruce (Laguna and San Juan Pueblo), our facilities planning coordinator, who introduced us to the authors; and to Alena Chalan (Cochiti Pueblo), my special assistant, who researched the cover photo with the tribal staff of Cochiti Pueblo, New Mexico. Finally, we are indebted to our partners at Ten Speed Press, especially owner Phil Wood and senior editor Holly Taines White, whose patience and support have been invaluable.

—W. Richard West, Jr.
(Southern Cheyenne and member of the Cheyenne and Arapaho
Tribes of Oklahoma)
Director, National Museum of the American Indian

INTRODUCTION

Among the most fundamental of any culture's traditions are those surrounding its cuisine. For American Indian people, local foods and traditional ways of preparing food have always been and remain important sources of spirituality and community. Native recipes likewise reflect the diversity and adaptability of indigenous cultures.

It is fitting, then, that *Foods of the Americas* arises out of our work with the Smithsonian's National Museum of the American Indian, which takes as a guiding principle the affirmation of Native values. Created in 1989 in collaboration with Native communities throughout North, Central, and South America, the museum reflects Native American cultures from the Native perspective. The goal of this collection of recipes, essays, and images is to provide a sense of the diverse landscapes, the basic flavors, and the strong, vital cultures that have together produced a truly indigenous American cuisine.

Native American groups have acquired intimate knowledge of the foods that surround them, and they have cultivated to the fullest the food sources nearest at hand. Plains Indian tribes used every part of the buffalo they hunted. Northwest Coast peoples developed myriad techniques for preserving year-round the salmon that crowded their rivers only during certain seasons. People of the wooded Northeast and Great Lakes regions created hundreds of recipes, both culinary and medicinal, for the nuts that grew around them in abundance. And with the cultivation of maize, beginning some seven to ten thousand years ago in Mexico, corn became the physical and spiritual foundation of most American Indian cultures.

Most people don't pay close attention to the origins of the foods they enjoy today. Many foods commonly found on our shelves are credited to European or Asian origin—*Irish* potatoes, *Italian* tomatoes, and *Thai* chiles. But all of these foods originated here in the Americas. Potatoes were domesticated and bred by pre-Inka civilizations. Tomatoes and chiles were widely grown throughout South, Central, and North America before the arrival of the *conquistadors.*

The Americas are also the source of turkey, buffalo, corn, squash, amaranth, wild rice, avocados, pineapple, papaya, sunflowers, Jerusalem artichokes (also called sunchokes), pecans, peanuts, cashews, black walnuts, hazelnuts, tapioca, chocolate, and vanilla. After 1492, America's native foods transformed most of the world's cuisines.

While precious metals and other spoils of the Conquest bolstered a sagging European economy in the fifteenth and sixteenth centuries, the foods of the Americas have endured as the true New World legacy. What would the *pomme de terre*, the French "apple of the earth," be if not the American potato? As anthropologist Jack Weatherford has noted, Italians might still be eating pasta sauces derived only from carrots and beets if New World tomatoes, sweet peppers, and zucchini squash hadn't appeared. The fire in Asian and East Indian cookery would not exist if it were not for the spark of American chiles.

Some would assign origins of an American cuisine to the first settlement of Europeans in the Americas. Yet Native people, indeed entire Indian civilizations, were present when Europeans first arrived in the Western Hemisphere. One of the oldest and most continuously inhabited regions in North America is located on the border of Washington and Oregon, on the Columbia River about ninety miles east of present-day Portland. Dating as far back as 6000 B.C., a grand bazaar and trade market was located at Celilo Falls. As many as five thousand people from indigenous and diverse cultures gathered year after year to trade, feast, and participate in games and religious ceremonies.

By the time Europeans arrived, some of the Western Hemisphere's vast cache of raw materials had already undergone sophisticated hybridization and was incorporated into Native cuisines. The peoples of the Americas were diverse in their use of locally available ingredients, but they shared many preparation techniques and cooking methods. From early times, in all corners of the Americas, Native people harvested both wild and cultivated foods and harnessed the sun's energy for the preservation of their foods. For centuries, indigenous peoples explored a variety of cooking methods, using water and fire for steaming, boiling, and baking.

American cuisines continue to evolve, yet certain dishes are prepared or served today in the same fashion as they were thousands of years ago. Roasted potatoes, guacamole, popcorn, and toasted peanuts are splendid examples of ancient food preparations that remain popular with little change. Present-day Quechua people, descendants of the Inka, continue their centuries-old work toward the hybridization of the perfect potato for all climates. Maya people from Mexico's

Yucatán Peninsula to El Salvador are still preparing and serving *recados,* the intense flavoring pastes that can be slathered over meats before steam-cooking them. The Hopi continue to prepare *piki* bread and blue corn dishes, which have changed little through the centuries. Narragansett fishermen are still tending lobster pots, the form of which originated thousands of years ago. Aleuts are digging razor clams much as did hundreds of generations of their ancestors.

Other American foods undoubtedly await global discovery. Highly perishable fruits and vegetables such as the avocado were largely unknown beyond their native regions until the advent of improved shipping practices. New technologies influence the use, availability, or practicality of foods in the home and could open the door to the widespread use of foods that now are only locally available. Wapato, or arrowhead root, once an American staple with potato-like uses, may again appear on tables if technology advances its practicality as a food crop. A resurgence of demand for heirloom varieties of produce may engender research for new, more effective means of distribution.

The recipes included in this cookbook represent modern cultures of the Americas—they do not attempt to describe the ethnobotany of American civilizations nor do they reproduce authentic tribal specialties. After learning the basics of each dish, you're encouraged to borrow the flavors of one culture and pair them with those of another, basing your selections on flavor compatibility. For example, a Oaxacan masa dumpling can be cooked with a Pueblo- or Zuni-style succotash. As you become familiar with pre-Columbian foods, you will begin to understand the interrelationship of the ingredients and how the cuisines of the various regions changed and expanded with increased trade between civilizations.

This cookbook is intended to celebrate the original foods of the Americas; the recipes are designed to perpetuate a truly American tradition. In bringing Native foods and preparations to the fore, we honor those who came before us and recognize the contributions of all indigenous peoples to our American cuisine.

Chapter One

Small Plates & Appetizers

≋ Zuni women grinding corn, circa 1922. Zuni Pueblo, New Mexico. (N13130)

The Americas are composed of more than thirty separate countries—from Canada to Argentina. In pre-Columbian days, however, those boundaries had no meaning. Trade routes extended from the Andean cultures of South America to the Northwest Coast cultures of Alaska. Great trade centers were established in the Columbia Plateau region (now Washington and Oregon states), the Mississippi River region, the Southwest region of the United States, and in Mexico City, the Yucatán Peninsula, Ecuador, and Peru.

Through trade, indigenous people shared their knowledge of food cultivation and preparation with one another. The early Hohokam people, whose culture flourished from approximately 300 B.C. to A.D. 1500 in what is now Arizona, are one example. The Hohokam were highly skilled farmers. The Hohokam introduced irrigation agriculture to the arid West, building hundreds of miles of canals to carry water from the Rio Verde, Salt, and other rivers to their fields of maize, beans, squash, and cotton around present-day Phoenix and Tucson. Their ideas and skills were adopted by other cultures.

In pre-Columbian Chile, the Atacamenos and Diaguitas farmed the northern desert. The fertile lands of central and southern Chile were originally populated by seminomadic people known as the Mapuche, the Pehuelche, and the Tehuelche. These people were part-time farmers and hunter-gatherers. Along the coastal regions were nomadic canoe sailors known as the Alakalufe, the Yaganes, and the now-extinct Ona. These early Chileans consumed native land animals and enjoyed the great bounty of the ocean. They also cultivated and cooked potatoes, quinoa, beans, llama, deer, guanaco (a member of the South American camel family), vicuña (a relation of the alpaca), and rhea (a giant flightless bird related to the ostrich). Wild mushrooms, chiles, and avocados are among the foods domesticated by those cultures.

Native foods with histories dating back many thousands of years, such as potatoes and sweet potatoes, inspired the development of some of the traditional and nontraditional recipes in this chapter.

POTATO CAKES |||

This recipe was inspired by a type of potato cake made throughout the former Inka Empire, from Ecuador to Argentina. Try these cakes with a few slices of crisply fried potatoes for added texture or with crunchy fried plantains. For an experience that transcends time, serve them with peanut sauce. Peanuts and potatoes were among the earliest crops developed in South America. This recipe offers a creative solution for using leftover mashed potatoes. ||| MAKES 6 CAKES

PEANUT SAUCE
MAKES 2 CUPS

1 large tomato

2 tablespoons paprika oil or annatto oil (page 210)

1 small white onion, minced

1 clove garlic, minced

1/2 cup natural chunky peanut butter

1/2 cup vegetable stock (page 207) or water

Pinch of sea or kosher salt

Pinch of freshly ground black pepper

Pinch of ground aji or cayenne pepper

4 russet potatoes, peeled and quartered

3 ramps or green onions, white part only, thinly sliced

Pinch of sea or kosher salt

Pinch of freshly ground black pepper

1 egg white

Masa harina or whole wheat flour, for dredging

Paprika oil or annatto oil, for cooking (page 210)

To prepare the sauce, prepare a hot fire in a charcoal grill, preheat a gas grill to high, or preheat the broiler. Place the tomato on the grill rack or in a broiler pan and cook, turning often, for 4 to 5 minutes, until the skin is slightly blackened and blistered. Peel the tomato and dice.

Heat the oil in a saucepan over medium heat. Add the onion and cook for 5 minutes, until transparent. Add the tomato and garlic and cook, stirring often, for 3 to 4 minutes. Add the peanut butter, stock, salt, pepper, and aji and cook, stirring often, for about 5 minutes, until the sauce is somewhat thick but pourable. The sauce may be stored for up to 2 weeks in the refrigerator and reheated, if desired.

Place the potatoes in a saucepan with water to cover. Bring to a boil over high heat, then decrease the heat to medium and simmer for about 15 minutes, until the potatoes are just tender when pierced with a fork. Drain the potatoes. Reserve 1 potato. Mash the remaining potatoes with a fork or pass through a food mill. Allow to cool completely.

Coarsely grate the reserved potato, cover, and set aside. Place the mashed potatoes in a bowl and add the ramps, salt, and pepper. Lightly whisk the egg white in a separate bowl. Add the egg white to the potatoes, and mix to incorporate evenly.

To form the cakes, divide the potato mixture into 6 equal portions. Shape each portion into a cake about 3 inches in diameter and 2 inches thick. Spoon about 1 teaspoon of the grated potato onto a work surface and place 1 of the formed cakes on the grated potato. Depress the cake firmly into the grated potato to coat the cake. Turn over and repeat with the other side of the cake. Repeat the process for the remaining cakes.

Sprinkle the cakes lightly with masa harina. Heat some of the oil in a sauté pan over medium heat. Add the cakes and cook, turning once, for about 7 minutes on each side, until nicely browned with a firm crust. Serve immediately with the peanut sauce on the side.

Mexican-Style Empanadas with Beef Picadillo

||| Empanadas are popular throughout Latin America, and the fillings are myriad. This northern-style empanada uses beef rather than the pork of central Mexico. Any meat may be used with your favorite flavorings. This preparation uses canela, or Mexican cinnamon. Picadillo usually contains almonds or some other type of nut. Empanadas offer a versatile way to use tantalizing leftovers, where a few cups of filling are sufficient for a delicious small course.

||| **MAKES 8 EMPANADAS**

BEEF PICADILLO
MAKES ABOUT 3 1/2 CUPS

1 tablespoon raisins

2 tablespoons corn oil

1 pound beef chuck or stew meat, cut into 1/4-inch cubes

1/2 cup minced white onion

1 jalapeño chile, seeded and minced

1 clove garlic, minced

1 tomato, diced, or 1 cup canned diced tomatoes

1 tablespoon tomato paste

1 bay leaf

2 small waxy potatoes, sliced

1 tablespoon cider vinegar

1-inch piece canela, or 1/4 teaspoon ground cinnamon

1/8 teaspoon ground allspice

3/4 teaspoon sea or kosher salt

1/8 teaspoon freshly ground black pepper

4 cups fresh masa or reconstituted masa harina (see tortilla recipe, page 153)

Corn oil, for frying

To make the filling, place the raisins in a bowl and add boiling water to cover. Let rest for 15 minutes, until plumped. Drain well.

Heat a heavy saucepan over high heat and add the oil. Add the meat and cook, stirring, for 5 to 7 minutes, until browned. Add the onion, jalapeño, and garlic and cook, stirring often, for about 4 minutes, until the vegetables are soft but not brown. Add the raisins, tomato, tomato paste, bay leaf, potatoes, vinegar, canela, allspice, salt, and pepper. Bring to a simmer and cook for about 30 minutes, until the meat and potatoes are tender. Remove from the heat and allow to cool. Remove and discard the piece of canela.

Line a baking sheet with plastic wrap. Separate the masa into 6 pieces and roll into balls. Press the balls in a metal or wooden tortilla press (available at most Latin American markets) or place between 2 sheets of plastic wrap or waxed paper and roll to about 5 inches wide by 1/8 inch thick. Spoon 2 tablespoons of the picadillo into the middle of each masa disk and fold over. Depress the seams firmly and crimp the edges to seal. Place on the prepared baking sheet and cover with a clean cloth to keep moist while assembling the remaining empanadas.

To cook, heat the oil in a heavy sauté pan over medium-low to medium heat. Place the empanadas, flat side down first, in the pan. Cook, turning once, for 5 minutes on each side, or until golden brown. Serve immediately.

EMPADAS |||

These meat pies are the Brazilian version of empanadas. Varieties are endless, but this version should provide you with a model for developing your own. Try substituting pork or chicken for the beef. Shrimp and other seafood are used extensively in Brazil, and to substitute here, simply reduce the cooking time for the seafood and add it at the last minute prior to assembling the *empadas*. *Empadinahs* are tiny pies baked in tartlet molds. If you prefer, divide the dough into smaller sizes and roll them out to 2 inches for a bite-sized version. ||| **MAKES ABOUT 12 EMPADAS**

DOUGH

3 cups unbleached all-purpose flour

1/2 cup plus 1 teaspoon vegetable shortening or unsalted butter

1 egg plus 1 egg white

1/2 teaspoon sea or kosher salt

1/2 cup cold water

FILLING

1 tomato

1 tablespoon corn oil

1 small white onion, minced

1 clove garlic, minced

1/2 pound ground beef

3/4 cup diced russet potato

1/4 teaspoon ground allspice

1 small chile, seeded and minced

1 bay leaf

1 teaspoon sea or kosher salt

Pinch of freshly ground black pepper

3/4 cup water or brown stock (page 208)

Flour, for dusting

1 egg

1 tablespoon water

Pinch of sea or kosher salt

To prepare the dough, place the flour in a bowl and add the shortening. Cut with a pastry cutter or the tines of a fork until the mixture resembles coarse meal. In a separate bowl, beat the egg with the egg white, salt, and water. Make a well in the center of the flour mixture and add the egg mixture. Work the egg into the flour with your fingers and knead the dough into a ball. Cover and refrigerate for at least 30 minutes. The dough keeps well for several days in the refrigerator.

To prepare the filling, prepare a hot fire in a charcoal grill, preheat a gas grill to high, or preheat the broiler. Place the tomato on the grill rack or in a broiler pan and cook, turning often, for 4 to 5 minutes, until the skin is slightly blackened and blistered. Peel the tomato and chop coarsely.

Heat a heavy-bottomed pot over medium heat. Add the oil, onion, and garlic and cook, without browning, for about 5 minutes. Add the tomato, beef, potato, allspice, chile, bay leaf, salt, pepper, and water. Cook, stirring often, for 15 to 20 minutes, until the meat is browned and cooked through and the liquid has nearly evaporated. Remove from the heat and allow to cool completely. Remove and discard the bay leaf.

Preheat the oven to 350°F. Lightly oil and flour a baking sheet or line with parchment paper.

To assemble the empadas, lightly flour a work surface. Cut the dough in half horizontally and cover one half with a clean kitchen towel to keep moist. Roll the other half of the dough out to about 1/8 inch thick. Cut into 12 squares or rounds about 3 1/2 inches wide. Place a generous tablespoon of the meat mixture in the center of each piece of dough. Roll out and cut the other portion of dough in the same manner. Whisk the egg with the water and salt to make an egg wash. Brush the edges of the bottom dough pieces with the egg wash. Top each with another dough piece and crimp the edges with the tines of a fork or your fingertips. Place the empadas on the prepared baking sheet. Brush the tops with the remaining egg wash. Bake for about 30 minutes, until golden brown. Serve warm.

VENEZUELAN AREPAS ||| *Arepas* are corn cakes made in Venezuela and Colombia. They are very simple to prepare and provide a basis for many variant dishes. The corn flour for this recipe can be found at most Latin American markets or be ordered by mail. The arepas may be served with Venezuelan fresh cream cheese, goat cheese, or crema (page 209). ||| MAKES 8 AREPAS

2 cups arepas corn flour or masa harina

1 teaspoon sea or kosher salt

About 2 cups water

Corn oil, for cooking

Preheat the oven to 350°F.

In a bowl, combine the flour, salt, and water, using enough water so that the dough is firm enough to hold its shape. Separate the dough into 8 pieces. Form each piece into a cake about $3^{1}/_{2}$ inches in diameter by $^{1}/_{3}$ inch thick.

Lightly oil a baking sheet. Heat some of the oil in a sauté pan over medium heat. Add the arepas and cook, turning once, for about 4 minutes on each side, until light brown. Transfer to the prepared baking sheet and finish cooking in the oven for about 20 minutes, turning over once or twice. To test for doneness, tap the cakes with your fingers; they should sound hollow. Serve immediately.

ROASTED CHILE POBLANO RELLENOS ||| In Central and South Amer-

ican kitchens, the aroma of roasting chiles is ever present. This preparation is a delicious way to use leftover beans and

sweet potatoes. Because *chiles poblanos* vary greatly in size, you may find yourself with some extra filling. Use this versa-

tile bean mixture for empanadas (page 5), enchiladas, or omelets. ||| Serve the chiles as a light lunch with crema

(page 209), or as a first course followed by Great Basin–Style Braised Rabbit (page 84). ||| MAKES 4 RELLENOS

4 poblano chiles

FILLING
2 tablespoons dried currants

1 sweet potato

3 tablespoons pine nuts

1 cup drained canned black beans

1/4 cup grated asadero cheese or Gouda
cheese

2 tablespoons ripe plantain, cut into
small dice

1/4 cup minced cilantro

1 chile chipotle en adobo, minced

1/2 teaspoon adobo sauce

1/3 teaspoon sea or kosher salt

1/4 teaspoon freshly ground black pepper

Corn oil, for cooking

3/4 cup queso fresco, ricotta cheese, or
fromage blanc

Place the chiles over an open gas flame or in a broiler. Cook, turning often, for 3 to 5 minutes, until evenly blackened. Place the chiles in a plastic bag and allow to steam for 5 minutes. When cool enough to handle, scrape away the skin with the tip of a knife. Keeping the stem attached and whole, make an incision in the chiles from the stem to about 1/2 inch away from the tip. Remove the seeds, keeping the chiles intact.

To prepare the filling, preheat the oven to 350°F. Place the currants in a bowl and add boiling water to cover. Let rest for 15 minutes, until plumped. Drain well. Place the sweet potato in the oven and roast for 20 to 30 minutes, until fork-tender. Remove from the oven and allow to cool. Increase the oven temperature to 400°F. When cool enough to handle, peel the sweet potato and cut into 1/4-inch cubes. Measure out 2 tablespoons for use in this recipe; reserve the remainder for another use.

Spread the pine nuts on a baking sheet and place in the oven. Toast for 6 to 8 minutes, until golden brown. Maintain the oven temperature at 400°F.

Place the currants, sweet potato, pine nuts, beans, asadero cheese, plantain, cilantro, chile chipotle, adobo sauce, salt, and pepper in a bowl. Stir with a wooden spoon to combine completely.

Lightly oil a baking dish with the corn oil. Spoon about 1 tablespoon of the queso fresco into each chile. Spoon about 1/2 cup of the bean mixture into each chile. Reshape the chiles to approximate their natural size, adding or removing filling as necessary, depending on the size of each chile. As you complete them, place the chiles in the prepared baking dish with the seams facing up.

Pour about 1/4 cup water into the baking dish. Tent the entire pan loosely with aluminum foil. Bake for about 15 minutes, until the filling is hot throughout. Slip the tip of a knife into a chile and leave it in the filling for a moment. If the tip is hot when removed, the chiles are ready. Serve immediately.

FRY BREAD TACOS ||| The ubiquitous fry bread taco served across the northern continent can be one of the most satisfying dishes when ingredients are selected at their prime and care is given to the preparation. The concept of sharing little dishes is a traditional approach to mealtime that lends itself to community and family interaction. While these toppings are atypical, they are adapted from traditional preparations. Two tacos make a nice meal on their own served with a salad or sliced ripe fruit. Pickled chiles can be found at Latin American markets or in the Latin American section of most supermarkets. ||| MAKES 8 TO 10 TACOS

1 recipe Fry or Grill Bread (page 150)

1 recipe Sonoran-Style Beef Deshebrada
  (page 79) or Beef Picadillo (page 5)

¼ cup crumbled cotija cheese or feta cheese

1 cup Fresh Mexican Tomato Salsa (page 30)

1 cup Corn and Chayote Relish (page 35)

1 cup Guacamole (page 11)

2 pickled chiles, sliced

1 cup shredded cabbage

Place the cooked bread on a serving platter. Divide the beef among the breads, distributing evenly. Sprinkle the cheese over the meat. Spoon some salsa on each taco, followed by some of the relish, guacamole, chiles, and cabbage. Serve immediately.

CHICKEN DESHEBRADA FRY BREAD TACOS: Substitute chicken for the beef (page 79).

FRY BREAD TACOS WITH BUFFALO CHILI: Substitute chili (page 68) for the beef.

GRILLED VEGETABLE GRILL BREAD TACOS: Grill whole summer squashes, onions, leeks, and tomatoes and cut into bite-sized pieces. Spoon hot black beans on the grill bread, followed by the vegetables. Top with salsa, corn relish, or guacamole.

SQUASH BLOSSOM GRILL BREAD TACOS: Dip squash blossoms in buttermilk, then dredge in cornmeal, and fry in about 1 inch of safflower oil heated in a heavy sauté pan. Cook, turning once, for about 1 minute on each side, until crisp and lightly browned. Drain on paper towels and serve on grill bread over sliced tomatoes, shredded lettuce, and Tomatillo and Pumpkin Seed Vinaigrette (page 46).

FRIED GREEN TOMATOES ||| Whether inclement weather leaves tomatoes unripe or the cook decides to use them before their prime, fried green tomatoes are simple to prepare. Eat them in early summer with simple grilled meats or as a delicious accompaniment to lightly seasoned trout. ||| SERVES 4

1 tablespoon corn oil

2 green tomatoes

1/2 cup fine- or medium-grind cornmeal

Pinch of sea or kosher salt

Pinch of freshly ground black pepper

Place the oil in a heavy sauté pan over medium heat. Slice the tomatoes and dredge both sides in the cornmeal. Place the tomatoes in the sauté pan and cook, turning once, for 1 to 2 minutes on each side, until lightly browned. Season the fried tomatoes with salt and pepper. Set the tomato slices on a paper towel to drain and serve immediately.

GUACAMOLE ||| A *molcajete* is a Mexican basalt mortar used for grinding or mashing foods and spices with its accompanying *tejolote,* or pestle. Using the molcajete to prepare guacamole produces a most delightful chunky texture, and the flavors are contained rather than lost on a cutting surface. Not only that, the mortar becomes a perfect serving bowl. ||| SERVES 4

2 tablespoons coarsely chopped cilantro

1 Roma tomato, coarsely chopped

2 avocados, peeled and pitted

Juice of 1/2 lime

1/4 teaspoon hot sauce

Pinch of sea or kosher salt

Pinch of freshly ground black pepper

Place the cilantro, tomato, avocados, lime juice, and hot sauce in a mortar. Work the mixture with a pestle until it is well blended but chunky. Season with salt and pepper to taste.

POTTED SMOKED SALMON ||| The Coast Salish peoples of British Columbia had a

tradition of reconstituting dried salmon from winter stores, which inspired this recipe. Here, toasted hazelnut oil is used in place of eulachon oil or grease. Eulachon, or candlefish, prized for its oil and once an important trade commodity, is still widely used among the peoples of the region. Eulachon oil is eaten in the same manner as Europeans eat butter. The flavor of toasted hazelnut oil, while not at all like that of eulachon oil, has a slightly similar effect on the palate. Serve with fresh Grill Bread (page 150), spoon over a Cattail Cake (page 165), or served slathered between Buckskin Cakes (page 159) and some watercress or miner's lettuce dressed with lemon juice and nut oil. ||| Prepare this recipe with a mortar and pestle or a food processor. When the dish is creamed by hand, it has a wonderful texture, which is lost with modern methods. ||| SERVES 4

1/3 cup unsalted butter, at room temperature, or eulachon oil

2 tablespoons hazelnut oil (omit if using eulachon oil)

2/3 cup boneless smoked salmon, flaked

1/4 teaspoon fine sea salt

Pinch of freshly ground black pepper

Juice of 1/2 lemon

2 juniper berries, finely minced

Cream the butter in a mortar with a rubber spatula or wooden spoon. Add the hazelnut oil and salmon. With a pestle, work the butter and oil into the salmon until it is smooth and creamy. Add the salt, pepper, lemon juice, and juniper. Fully incorporate the seasonings and spoon the mixture into a decorative bowl to serve. Because the fish is smoked, potted salmon keeps well for up to a month if covered tightly and refrigerated.

POKE |||

Hawaiian poke refers to a traditional food and the manner in which it is cut—in small pieces. Traditionally, poke was made of reef fish served raw, but today it is made of a variety of fish, sometimes cooked. All kinds of tuna—yellowfin, bluefin, bigeye, skipjack, and albacore—are very good for this recipe. The fish must be absolutely fresh and of the highest quality. *Limu kohu* or *ogo*, types of seaweed, are traditionally used, but you can substitute reconstituted *kombu*, or kelp, which are widely available in the Asian section of supermarkets. *Inamona* is made from ground candlenuts (*kukui*) and the local salt that is mixed with a red-colored earth containing iron. Candlenuts can be found in East Indian and Asian markets. ||| SERVES 6

½ cup limu kohu, ogo, kombu, or thinly sliced green onions, white part only

1 pound tuna fillets, trimmed and cut into ½-inch pieces

1 tablespoon Hawaiian salt or sea salt

1 tablespoon finely chopped candlenuts or macadamia nuts, or 1 tablespoon sesame oil

Potato or taro chips, for serving

Bring a saucepan full of water to a boil over high heat. Add the limu kohu and submerge for 1 minute. Immediately drain in a colander and run under cold water. Squeeze out any excess water and transfer to a cutting board. Chop the seaweed coarsely.

Place the fish in a bowl with the limu kohu, salt, and candlenuts. Toss gently, cover, and refrigerate for 4 to 6 hours to let the flavors develop. Serve with the chips.

POKE WITH PEPPERS: Add ¼ red bell pepper, thinly sliced; ¼ small red onion, thinly sliced; 1 clove garlic, minced; pinch of crushed red peppers; and 1 tablespoon soy sauce. Decrease the amount of salt to ½ teaspoon.

WILD RICE AND CORN FRITTERS ||| The Chippewa have a symbiotic rela-

tionship with wild rice, assisting in its cultivation, harvesting, and preparation. Some Native people continue the cen-

turies-old method of harvesting rice by paddling into the fields in canoes and gently shaking the rice from the stalks

into baskets. These fritters are particularly good with Wild Ginger Dipping Sauce (page 36) or served with Imu-Style

Salmon (page 131). The fritters are lacy, so you may need to add a little more flour if the batter is too loose. |||

MAKES ABOUT 16 FRITTERS

1/2 cup wild rice

1 1/2 cups water

1 1/2 teaspoons sea or kosher salt

2 teaspoons baking powder

2 tablespoons cornstarch

1/4 cup whole wheat or cattail flour

1/8 teaspoon cayenne pepper

1 cup fresh corn kernels (1 large ear)

4 green onions, white part only, thinly sliced

2 eggs

1/4 cup beer

1/4 cup freshly grated Parmesan cheese
   (optional)

Safflower oil, for frying

In a bowl, rinse the rice in a few changes of fresh water, and strain. In a saucepan, bring the water and 1/2 teaspoon of the salt to a boil over high heat. Add the rice and cover loosely to allow the steam to escape. Decrease the heat to a slow simmer and cook for about 35 minutes, until tender. Add water as necessary to keep the rice covered throughout cooking. Remove from the heat, drain, and allow to cool completely.

To make the fritters, place the remaining 1 teaspoon salt, baking powder, cornstarch, and flour in a bowl. Stir with a fork to combine. Add the rice, cayenne, corn, and green onions and stir well. Place the eggs in a separate bowl and whisk with a fork. Add the beer and beat well. Fold the egg mixture into the rice mixture with a rubber spatula, sprinkling the Parmesan cheese over the batter while folding.

To cook the fritters, heat 1 inch of oil in a heavy saucepan over medium-high heat. When a small drop of the batter sizzles, the oil is ready for cooking. Using 2 soup spoons, slip spoonfuls of the batter into the hot oil, using 1 spoon to slide the batter off of the other. Leave plenty of space between the fritters to allow even cooking. Cook for 5 to 6 minutes, until the bottoms are golden brown, then use a slotted spoon or tongs to turn the fritters. Cook the other side for 5 to 6 minutes, until golden brown and a knife inserted into the center comes out clean. Transfer the cooked fritters to a tray lined with paper towels and keep warm while cooking the remaining batter. The fritters may be kept in a warm oven for up to 10 minutes. Serve warm.

Corn Is Life

ONE OF MY FAVORITE HOPI FOODS is *tupevu,* freshly roasted sweet corn. In late summer, after the harvest, many Hopi households prepare to roast sweet corn. The roasting of sweet corn is usually done once a year, to cook and preserve a full harvest to be used throughout the year. Sweet corn is the only kind of Hopi corn that is cooked in this way: steamed in a sealed pit. The pit is roughly three to four feet wide and can be about six feet deep. It's big enough to hold a whole truckload of corn.

The day before cooking, while the pit is being heated with fire for several hours, two perfect ears of corn are sought. When found they are prepared in a special way to represent the mother corn and father corn. When the fire has died down, the mother corn is

PHOTO © JOHN HARRINGTON AND SMITHSONIAN INSTITUTION

≈ Harvested Hopi corn of different colors set out to dry.

placed in the pit first, at the bottom. Then the hundreds of ears of corn from the year's harvest are thrown into the pit. The father corn is added last to the top of the pile. The pit is then sealed with mud so the heat cannot escape. The heat within the pit will release the natural moisture found between the husks and kernels, steaming the corn neatly within its husk. We have to wait until the morning of the next day for the corn to be ready.

It is told that when we, the Hopi, arrived at the place we now live, corn kernels and a planting stick were the only things given to us for our survival. Therefore, corn to Hopi people literally represents life, and the use of it within Hopi culture is ubiquitous.

Dry farming is still practiced at Hopi. Planting and maintaining a cornfield usually begins in the early spring and is done by Hopi men, mostly by hand. In spring they work to keep the field free of weeds and rodents. As the plants sprout through the dry sand, these seedlings represent new life, such as children. Throughout the summer months, the men laboriously care for them as such, hoeing weeds sometimes daily, singing to the corn plants, praying for their continued life and growth, and praying for the moisture that is needed in the arid landscape of Hopi. Once harvested, the corn becomes the property of their wives or mothers. It is they who will preserve, prepare, and use it throughout the year for meals and ceremony.

Corn serves as the main staple, with many different dishes and breads made from it. Besides sweet corn, the other kinds of corn planted by the Hopi are blue, white, red, purple, yellow, and speckled, which is a combination of several colors. Corn is also symbolic of the various cardinal directions. A perfect ear will represent the spiritual mother of a new baby, or a new initiate in a ceremony. White corn is ground into a coarse meal and ritually prepared for use in prayer. Finely ground meal from roasted sweet corn is called *toosi* and is mixed with water to create *qömi,* a baked dough that is especially important for an unmarried girl and her family because it will be used in the girl's engagement ceremony. Large amounts of blue and white cornmeal are used when a woman gets married in a traditional Hopi wedding.

Before the sun has risen the next day, along with others in my family, I awake and go outside our house, bleary-eyed and chilled. We hover around the pit to warm ourselves. The smell of the sweet corn, the smoke left over from the fire, and the early morning air rouse me. The seal of the pit is broken, and the father corn is retrieved. When its husks are peeled back, everyone gathers to take a bite of the father corn. This corn ritual creates what it is meant to: an increase of appetite and a renewal of strength. But coming together to share this one ear of corn also signifies family unity and is meant to eliminate any divisiveness.

Soon the men begin to empty the pit of corn, taking turns jumping into the pit as the hole deepens. They sometimes compete to see who can stay in the longest and retrieve the most corn. It is fun to see them get sweaty from the heat and black from the soot, each trying to outdo the other. Outside the pit, the mound of steaming corn grows larger, until finally the mother corn is retrieved. I join the others to repeat the shared eating of the mother corn, knowing that this signifies the strength of both parents to a family. Finally, we are allowed to pick a full ear for ourselves. My hands turn black from the charred husks as I peel back each layer. The heat rises off the cob and my hands are warmed

as I take a small piece to personally feed the spirits. As the early morning light slowly turns into full daylight, I eat to my heart's content, enjoying the smoky sweetness.

Askwali (thank you)!

—Susan Secakuku

Susan Secakuku (Hopi) was born and raised on the Hopi reservation in Arizona. She is a member of the Hopi Butterfly Clan. She received her B.S. from Arizona State University and her M.A. in Museum Studies from George Washington University. She worked for six years in the Community Services department of the National Museum of the American Indian. Now based in the Hopi community, she is an independent consultant who works with Native American tribes on museum operations and cultural projects.

≈ Susan Secakuku's father, Ferrell Secakuku, checks his corn plants at the beginning of harvest time.

CLAM AND CORNMEAL FRITTERS ||| These traditional fritters are typical

fare of tribes in the southeastern United States, where clams are abundant. They are very good on their own, with a

small salad of watercress in nut oil and lemon juice, or dipped in a sauce. ||| MAKES ABOUT 24 FRITTERS

2¹/₂ pounds clams

1 teaspoon sea or kosher salt

2 eggs

¹/₂ cup milk

1 cup unbleached all-purpose flour

¹/₂ cup white cornmeal or johnny meal

1 teaspoon baking powder

2 tablespoons rendered bacon fat
    or safflower oil

1 green onion, white part only, thinly sliced

Pinch of freshly ground black pepper

Corn oil, for frying

Rinse the clams by placing them in a bowl and submerging in cold water. Remove and discard any open clams. Transfer to a large saucepan and add 2 to 3 inches of cold water and the salt. Place the pan over medium-high heat. Cover and bring to a boil. Decrease the heat to medium-low and cook until the clams have opened, about 10 to 12 minutes. Remove and discard any clams that do not open. Strain the liquid and reserve ¹/₂ cup for the fritter batter. Remove the cooked clams from the shells and discard the shells. Chop the clams finely and allow to cool completely.

Beat the eggs in a bowl with the reserved clam cooking liquid and the milk. In a separate bowl, mix the flour, cornmeal, baking powder, and a pinch of salt. Add the flour mixture to the egg mixture and beat with a wooden spoon until well blended. Add the bacon fat, green onion, pepper, and chopped clams to the batter. Stir to fully incorporate.

Heat 1 inch of oil in a heavy sauté pan over medium-high heat. Drop the batter by tablespoonfuls into the oil, a few at a time. Do not overcrowd the pan. Fry the fritters, turning once, for 6 to 7 minutes on each side, until brown. With a slotted spoon, transfer to a tray lined with paper towels and keep warm while cooking the remaining batter. Serve warm.

CHOCHOYOTES

||| While working in her home in Zitácuaro, Mexico, Diana Kennedy served these *chochoyote* dumplings to complement a flavorful, brothy Oaxacan stew. They are traditionally served in Oaxacan moles or black beans, and also complement many nontraditional vegetarian dishes such as Three Sisters Stew (page 70). Asiento is the substance remaining after making *chicharrón*, rendering pork fat. It is widely available in Oaxaca but is not easily found in the United States. ||| SERVES 4

3 cups brown stock (page 208) or vegetable stock (page 207)

1 cup fresh masa or reconstituted masa harina (see tortilla recipe, page 153)

2 tablespoons asiento or lard

¼ teaspoon sea or kosher salt

Place the stock in a large saucepan over medium-high heat and bring to a simmer.

In a bowl, combine the masa, asiento, and salt to form a smooth dough. Divide the dough into 16 equal portions. Roll each piece into a ball and, using your thumb, make an impression about halfway through each ball.

Place the dumplings in the simmering stock and cover the pan. Decrease the heat to low and simmer for 15 to 17 minutes, until the dumplings have expanded by half the original size and appear opaque and cooked throughout. Ladle into soup bowls and serve immediately.

TAMALES

BASIC PREPARATION AND STEAMING

TAMALE IS THE TERM USED to describe a cornhusk- or banana leaf–wrapped package that is filled with masa dough, meats, and flavorings. The *nacatamale* is a Nicaraguan and Guatemalan tamale made of masa and flavorings that are wrapped in banana leaves and boiled. The *hallaca* is a Venezuelan or Colombian tamale, made using a similar technique and resembling Peruvian tamales. These tamales were probably introduced into South America from Central America. The *humita* is a tamale made from fresh corn. It is prepared from Ecuador to Argentina.

All tamales and tamale-like preparations like humitas and hallacas involve the same basic steps for assembly and cooking. A steamer must first be selected and readied. Types of steamers used by regional cooks vary. A heavy-bottomed pot with a perforated steam insert and tight-fitting lid works best. Many variations of steamers exist, from a cake rack or vegetable steamer insert placed in the bottom of the pan and covered with aluminum foil to steamers designed specifically for tamales. Asian-designed bamboo steamers may be used, but the entire assembly must be tightly housed in foil as this type of steamer allows too much steam to escape to efficiently cook the tamales. The aluminum-encased bamboo steamer makes it difficult to check for doneness. Cooking time must be extended if you choose such a steamer. Be thorough in inspecting for a good seal if you determine that the tamales require more time.

Prepare the steamer prior to cooking and have the water temperature near boiling to expedite the process. To help avoid simmering the steamer dry, drop a penny in the bottom portion when you add water. The penny gently rattles when the water is simmering. If you no longer hear the penny rattle, add more water—your pot is dry.

BASIC TAMALES |||

This recipe approximates the tamales typical of central Mexico and, though untraditional, produces a very high-quality and fine cake-like tamale. If you want to replicate the original textures and flavors of authentic tamales, Diana Kennedy's excellent treatise on the subject in her classic cookbook, *The Art of Mexican Cooking*, is highly recommended. While lard is the standard fat used throughout Mexico, you'll also get wonderful flavor by using some of the rendered fat from the meat used to make the tamales. Cornhusks can be purchased in the Latin American section of most markets. ||| MAKES 15 TO 16 TAMALES

1 cup vegetable shortening, butter, or lard, or rendered chicken, duck, or goose fat

2½ cups fresh masa or reconstituted masa harina (see tortilla recipe, page 153)

1 teaspoon sea or kosher salt

¾ cup chicken brown stock (page 208), water, or other complementary broth

25 to 30 dried cornhusks, submerged in tepid water for at least 2 hours or overnight

1 recipe Sonoran-Style Beef Deshebrada (page 79) or beef picadillo (page 5)

Place the shortening in a bowl and beat with an electric mixer on high speed until doubled in volume. In a separate bowl, mix the masa, salt, and chicken stock together. With the mixer on medium speed, add walnut-sized portions of the masa mixture one at a time into the shortening until all of the masa is incorporated, beating continuously to form a smooth, light batter. The batter is ready when a small amount floats when dropped into water.

To assemble the tamales, drain the cornhusks and pat dry. Select the larger husks for the tamales. Lay out 2 or 3 husks and spoon about 4 generous tablespoons of the dough on each husk. With the back of a moist spoon, tamp the dough to within 1 inch of the sides and 2 inches from the top and bottom, to allow for expansion. Spread 4 tablespoons of the deshebrada over the masa. Fold the sides of the husk over the filling. Fold the bottom of the cornhusk up to close the bottom edge, leaving the top open. Repeat the process for all of the tamales.

To cook the tamales, place some of the smaller, unused husks in the bottom of a steamer and stand the tamales upright on top of them with the unfolded, exposed end facing upward. Lean the tamales against each other until they stand against the walls of the steamer without support. Place wet cornhusks over the top of the tamales to lock in the heat and moisture and centralize the cooking. Cover the steamer and place over high heat. Steam over simmering water for about 1 hour, until the husks come away clean from the tamale dough.

Tamales freeze well. If you make a large batch for later use, place the uncooked tamales in a tightly sealed plastic bag and stand upright in the freezer. Cook the tamales unthawed, adding 20 to 30 minutes to the cooking time.

HALLACAS ||| As with tamales, the *hallacas* of Venezuela and Colombia have as many fillings as there are cooks. This filling is a standard that you will find prepared in various ways throughout those regions, although rendered pork fat is almost always used. Other meats work well with these flavorings, or make them meatless by substituting sweet potatoes, plantains, and nuts. The filling may be made up to a few days prior to assembling. Hallacas freeze well. Cook the hallacas unthawed, and add 30 minutes to the cooking time. Serve hallacas with a cool Chayote Salad (page 36), sliced fresh pineapple, and star apple. ||| MAKES 8 HALLACAS

FILLING

1/4 cup raisins

1/2 cup water

2 tablespoons corn oil

1/2 pound boneless pork shoulder or country-style ribs, cut into 1/2-inch cubes

1/2 pound beef round or chuck, cut into 1/2-inch cubes

1/2 teaspoon sea or kosher salt

1/2 teaspoon freshly ground black pepper

1/4 teaspoon crushed red peppers

4 cloves garlic, minced

1 white onion, minced

1 green bell pepper, minced

1 (14 1/2-ounce) can diced tomatoes, drained

1/2 cup white stock (page 209)

1/2 cup brown stock (page 208)

2 tablespoons minced flat-leaf parsley

2 tablespoons capers, drained

8 stuffed green olives with pimientos, sliced

To prepare the filling, place the raisins in a small saucepan and cover with the water. Bring to a boil over high heat and then immediately cover and remove from the heat.

Heat a heavy saucepan over medium-high heat and add the oil. Add the pork and beef to the pan and cook, stirring often, for 10 to 12 minutes, until browned on all sides. Add the salt, pepper, red peppers, garlic, onion, and green pepper and cook, stirring often, for about 10 minutes, until the vegetables are soft but not brown. Add the tomatoes, white stock, brown stock, and the plumped raisins with their liquid. Bring the mixture to a boil and then decrease the heat to medium-low. Simmer for 30 to 60 minutes, until the meat is fork-tender. Allow to cool slightly.

To make the dough, place the hominy in a blender or a food mill and grind to a medium coarseness. (A mortar and pestle works best for this but takes some elbow grease.) Place the milled hominy in a bowl and add the shortening, salt, and annatto oil. Blend with a rubber spatula until the mixture is smooth and completely incorporated. Scrape the dough out onto a clean surface with the spatula. Knead for several minutes until it is smooth and pliant.

To assemble the hallacas, lay out 8 of the banana leaf pieces. From the remaining leaf, tear 8 thin pieces to use for ties. Spoon about 1/4 cup of the dough onto each banana leaf. Depress the dough with slightly moistened fingers to form a 1/4-inch-thick rectangle about 4 by 5 inches. Place about 1/4 cup of the meat mixture in the center of the dough. Sprinkle with the parsley, capers, and olives.

DOUGH

1 (13-ounce) can white hominy, drained and rinsed

1 tablespoon vegetable shortening or unsalted butter

Pinch of sea or kosher salt

1 tablespoon plus 1 teaspoon annatto oil (page 210)

9 (8 by 8-inch) pieces banana leaf

Fold each hallaca by turning up the bottom edge of the leaf, with the natural grain of the leaf over the filling, and turning down the top edge to overlap the bottom. Fold the right edge in and close the package with the left edge. Tie the hallaca around the center to secure. After assembling, place in the top of a steamer and steam over high heat for about 1 hour, until the dough comes away clean from the banana leaf. Serve immediately.

HUMITAS ||| These South American fresh corn tamales provide a wonderful foil for the rich, natural juices of Roast Wild Turkey (page 112). They may also be served as a first course. ||| MAKES ABOUT 16 HUMITAS

3 cups fresh corn kernels (4 ears), with husks reserved

2 eggs

3 tablespoons unsalted butter, melted

2 teaspoons unbleached all-purpose flour

1/2 teaspoon sea or kosher salt

1/8 teaspoon ground chile powder

Place the corn in a blender or food processor. Pulse until the kernels resemble a coarse meal. Crack the eggs into a bowl and whisk until completely blended. Add the corn to the eggs and combine thoroughly. Add the butter, flour, salt, and ground chile. Whisk until the mixture is fully incorporated.

To assemble the humitas, tear 1 cornhusk into thin lengths for use as ties. Lay 1 large or 2 smaller overlapping cornhusks together. Spoon about 2 tablespoons of the corn mixture into the center of the cornhusks. Fold in all sides of the husk to make a little package. Tie the bundle with 1 piece of torn husk. Assemble the remaining humitas. Lay in rows in the top portion of a steamer, alternating them in crisscross fashion to evenly distribute the weight. Cover the steamer and place over high heat. Steam over simmering water for about 50 minutes, until the filling is opaque. Serve immediately.

CHAPTER TWO

COLD SAUCES, RELISHES, & SALADS

≋ View of Zuni (Paquin family?) waffle gardens, 1919. New Mexico. (P11433)

25

Until they began to master cultivation about seven thousand years ago, early peoples of the Americas foraged and hunted their foods. Their diets were dictated by the season, and through trial and error they distinguished between plants that were edible and those that could be used for medicinal and other purposes. Many of the edible foods discovered by ancient peoples remain popular, but some important ones have been lost to industrialization. Others, such as camas root or wapato, still exist but are not readily available. They are eaten only during celebrations and ceremonies.

Fresh garden vegetables, fruits, and foraged foods have always been important to Native people. Unlike most European-American menus, which feature salad before or after the main course, indigenous meals integrated salad into the overall menu in the form of relishes, condiments, or flavorings. Still, cultural diversification has influenced the way all people of the Western Hemisphere eat; therefore, salads are taking a more prominent role in today's menu planning for the American Indian table.

CHILTOMATE SAUCE |||

This recipe of the ancient Maya still accompanies many dishes found throughout Mexico's Yucatán Peninsula. The early people of the Yucatán processed this sauce in a wooden mortar, called a *kokoic*. Habañero chiles are found throughout the Yucatán. Considered to be among the hottest chiles, they also are beautifully colored and have a wonderful flavor. Habañeros are now usually available in markets throughout the Western Hemisphere when in season. If unavailable, substitute Scotch bonnet or any other hot chile. This recipe produces a full-flavored sauce with rustic texture. Serve this sauce warm with tacos or Hallacas (page 22).

||| MAKES ABOUT 2 CUPS

3 tomatoes, halved

1 habañero chile, seeded and coarsely chopped

1 clove garlic, coarsely chopped

½ tablespoon corn oil

½ white onion, thinly sliced

⅛ teaspoon sea or kosher salt

Heat a cast-iron skillet over medium-high heat. Lightly oil the tomatoes and place them skin side down in the skillet. Fry for 10 to 12 minutes, until browned and the skins are softened. Allow the tomatoes to cool completely. Place in a mortar or a blender with the chile and garlic and process to a coarse texture.

Heat the oil in a sauté pan over medium-high heat. Add the onion and cook for 4 to 5 minutes, until translucent. Do not let the onion brown. Add the tomato mixture, and cook for about 15 minutes, until the liquid evaporates. Stir in the salt. Serve warm.

FRESH TOMATILLO SALSA ||| This fresh green tomatillo sauce is a staple through-

out central Mexico. A version of the salsa is offered on most tables and in market stall eateries alongside the more familiar tomato salsa. Tomatillos vary greatly in size, depending on whether they are garden- or commercially grown, and on whether they originate in Mexico or the United States. Fifteen to twenty-five tomatillos may constitute a pound in Mexico compared with eight to twelve commercially grown tomatillos per pound in the United States. |||

MAKES ABOUT 1 3/4 CUPS

6 to 8 tomatillos (about 1/2 pound), husked

1/2 white onion, chopped

2 tablespoons coarsely chopped cilantro

2 serrano chiles, seeded and minced

Juice of 1 lime

Pinch of sea or kosher salt

Place the tomatillos in a saucepan and cover with water. Bring just to a simmer over medium-high heat, and cook for 5 to 10 minutes depending on the size, until soft. Do not boil. Take care to turn the tomatillos often and avoid bursting the skins. Drain, reserve the juice, and allow the tomatillos to cool.

Place the onion, cilantro, chiles, lime juice, and salt in a *molcajete* (a Mexican basalt mortar), food processor, or blender. Grind or process the ingredients until a coarse-textured paste forms with bits of cilantro and chile still visible. Transfer the paste to a bowl. Place the tomatillos in the mortar or food processor and repeat the grinding process, adding some of the reserved cooking liquid to ease the process and thin the tomatillos to the consistency of heavy cream. Add the tomatillos to the paste and mix well with a spoon, adding more liquid if necessary. The salsa can be prepared up to a few hours prior to serving, though it is best eaten soon after preparation. It will hold for 1 to 2 days if tightly covered and refrigerated.

≈ Marketplace in Santa Cruz, Oaxaca, 1999.

PHOTO © ROBERTO YSAIS AND SMITHSONIAN INSTITUTION

Fresh Mexican Tomato Salsa ||| This is the ubiquitous red salsa

enjoyed throughout Mexico and now most of the Northern Hemisphere. There is no substitute for making sauce with vine-ripened fresh tomatoes grown in soil. Consider nothing less for this and all raw tomato sauces and salsas.

||| MAKES ABOUT 2 1/2 CUPS

2 ripe tomatoes, cored and finely chopped
(about 2 cups)

1/2 small white onion, finely chopped
(about 1/2 cup)

1/2 bunch cilantro, stemmed and coarsely
chopped (about 1/4 cup)

1 serrano chile, minced

Juice of 1 lime

1 tablespoon corn oil

Combine all of the ingredients in a bowl and mix well. For best results, prepare just before serving.

Roasted Tomatillo Salsa ||| Use this salsa as a dip with tortilla chips, serve it

with grilled meats and fish, or offer it as an accompaniment to Latin-inspired menus. ||| MAKES ABOUT 2 1/2 CUPS

2 green onions, white and green parts,
thinly sliced

2 serrano chiles, seeded

1/2 white onion, quartered

6 to 8 tomatillos (about 1/2 pound), husked

2 tablespoons finely chopped cilantro

1/4 teaspoon sea or kosher salt

Prepare a hot fire in a charcoal grill or preheat a gas grill to high.

Place the green onions, chiles, white onion, and tomatillos on the grill rack. Cook the green onions for 2 to 3 minutes, until charred and soft. Cook the chiles for 3 to 5 minutes, until charred but still firm. Cook the white onion and tomatillos for 5 to 7 minutes, turning often, until slightly charred and soft.

Transfer the grilled vegetables to a food processor or blender and blend until smooth. Transfer to a bowl and allow to cool completely. Add the cilantro and salt, stirring to incorporate completely. Serve at once.

QUINOA SALAD ||| Quinoa, a grain, was a major agricultural commodity of the Aztec and Inka. It is highly nutritious, very tasty, and easy to prepare. Try using quinoa as an alternative starch. Quinoa can be served hot with butter or nut oil and your favorite flavorings as an accompaniment to any meal. This salad is particularly good when sandwiched in lettuce leaves. ||| SERVES 6 TO 8

2 cups quinoa, rinsed and drained

1 large tomato, finely chopped

1 small red bell pepper, minced

1/2 cup fresh corn kernels or canned white hominy, drained and rinsed

1/2 cup coarsely chopped cilantro

1/4 cup minced fresh mint

1 teaspoon minced garlic

3 tablespoons corn oil

3 tablespoons sherry vinegar

Juice of 1 lime

1/4 teaspoon sea or kosher salt

1/4 teaspoon freshly ground black pepper

Bring a large saucepan of water to a boil over high heat and add the quinoa. Return to a boil, then decrease the heat to medium and simmer for about 10 minutes. The quinoa is cooked when all of the grains appear translucent. Drain the quinoa through a fine-mesh strainer, transfer to a baking sheet, and spread out with a fork. Allow to cool completely.

Transfer the quinoa to a bowl and add the tomato, bell pepper, corn, cilantro, mint, garlic, oil, vinegar, lime juice, salt, and pepper. Toss well and serve immediately.

Community Gardens and the Cycle of Life

AS IT HAS FOR HUNDREDS OF YEARS, early spring brings farmers out to their crops in southern Arizona's Salt River Valley. The earliest of these farmers, the Hohokam, who inhabited the region from about 200 B.C. to A.D. 1450, are recognized today as among North America's first cultivators of corn. Like many pre-Contact farmers, they planted small plots of land around their dwellings, using harvests from a variety of plants for medicinal and ceremonial purposes as well as to enrich their diet. Larger Hohokam fields were irrigated by a canal system that covered hundreds of miles. Today you can still see some of these ancient irrigation canals in the Gila and Salt River valleys. Just as the canals have endured, new generations of farmers and gardeners still cultivate the desert landscape.

The Hohokam fade from the archaeological record about a century before the Spanish arrival in the region, but many of their fields and gardens survived under the care of their descendants, the Pima-speaking Akimel O'odham, who continue to inhabit this seemingly inhospitable low desert region of high temperatures, drought, and flood.

Throughout North America, the earliest of our peoples survived in an environment that supported many more plant and animal species than it does today. Many groups were semi-sedentary, maintaining a diet of rabbit, turkey, and various rodents in addition to the occasional deer, elk, bighorn sheep, or javelina from the mountains. These semi-sedentary peoples also supplemented their diets with seasonal harvests of the local flora that grew by the perennial rivers and their tributaries.

As human populations increased, trade and technology flourished. In the early sixteenth century, European explorers noticed multiple varieties of plants in cultivation throughout the Western Hemisphere. The early farmers of North and South America experimented extensively with seeds and planting techniques. The farmers of the Southwest had numerous varieties of corn, beans, and squash, which they grew at specific times and locales. Trade played an important role in the dissemination of these early cultigens, many of which are still in use in present-day Native society.

Many aspects of Native American life were not separated from the whole, and the garden was part of a broader cycle of seasonal activities. Farming and gardening, like many facets of early Native American life, was community based and integrated with other aspects of tribal culture. From the garden came not only sustenance but also medical, ceremonial, utilitarian, and recreational commodities. Above all, the gifts from the garden reinforced the coherence of the community and encouraged a general contentment seldom seen today. The benefits of the garden are unequivocal: it sustains life, allows for a diverse menu, and, most important, promotes community balance and harmony.

Coerced away from our gardens and the values they instill, our lives have seen enormous change during the past several generations, yet the insight our ancestors gained through the millennia is vital to maintaining our mental and physical health. In today's Native communities, the concept of the community garden is making a comeback, as well as the idea of sustaining a biodiversity that is vital to our restoring our mental and physical health. The Gila Crossing community school, located in the Gila River Indian community, encourages healthy diets by growing several gardens around the campus. The students of the school then deliver the produce to community centers for the elderly. They also promote Native plants by distributing seedlings to nearby communities.

The garden not only promotes a healthy community but also contributes to a well-balanced diet. In addition, a diverse garden supports an ecologically sustainable environment in a world of finite resources. The Native population of this land has not disappeared and neither have the gardens or food they nurtured.

—Marcus Monenerkit

Marcus Monenerkit (Comanche) was born in Lawton, Oklahoma, and received his B.A. in Anthropology from Wichita State University. He is the associate registrar at the Heard Museum in Phoenix, where he helps raise the museum's Native foods garden.

≈ Marcus Monenerkit in the native plants garden at the Heard Museum, Phoenix, Arizona, May 2002. In the garden, museum staffers grow crops that are indigenous to the region, such as corn, tomatoes, squash, chile peppers, and Pima cotton.

WILD PLUM CATSUP ||| This unusual and tasty condiment is great with simple grilled

meats and fowl, such as venison, buffalo, and duck. Substitute domesticated plums or prunes if wild plums are unavailable. Most stone fruit works well with this recipe. ||| MAKES ABOUT 2 CUPS

1 pound ripe plums, halved and pitted

1/4 cup water

1 1/3 cups pure maple syrup

1/3 cup apple cider vinegar

1/2 teaspoon freshly ground cinnamon
   or canela

1/2 teaspoon freshly ground nutmeg

1/4 teaspoon freshly ground cloves

1/2 teaspoon sea or kosher salt

1/4 teaspoon freshly ground black pepper

Place the plums in a heavy nonreactive pan. Add the water and bring to a rolling boil over high heat. Decrease the heat to medium and simmer, stirring occasionally, for 15 to 20 minutes, until the plums are tender.

Allow the fruit to cool slightly and then pass through a food mill or strainer. Return the fruit purée to a saucepan over medium-high heat. Add the syrup, vinegar, cinnamon, nutmeg, cloves, salt, and pepper and bring to a boil. Decrease the heat to medium-low and simmer for about 20 minutes, until it is the consistency of heavy cream. Allow to cool and then refrigerate until completely chilled. Covered and refrigerated, the catsup will keep for 2 to 3 weeks.

ELDERBERRY CATSUP ||| The Quinault call these berries *k'lo manix*. Most indigenous people

of North America have many uses for both blue and red elderberries. While elderberries must be cooked prior to consumption, they are a prodigious source of vitamin C. Canela is a type of mild, soft cinnamon that grates easily. Any cinnamon may be substituted, but since the flavors of other types of cinnamon are usually more assertive, use about one-third less than the recipe calls for. Serve this unusual sauce with any roasted meat. ||| MAKES ABOUT 2 1/4 CUPS

4 cups elderberries, currants, or blueberries

2 cups apple cider vinegar

1/2 cup maple or turbinado sugar

1/2 teaspoon ground canela or cinnamon

1/2 teaspoon ground juniper berries

1 1/2 teaspoons ground allspice

1 1/2 teaspoons ground cloves

Pinch of crushed red peppers

Place the berries and vinegar in a heavy saucepan over medium-high heat. Bring to a rapid boil and then decrease the heat to medium. Simmer for 12 to 15 minutes, until the berries open. Pass through a food mill or strainer.

Return the berry purée to the pan and add the sugar, canela, juniper, allspice, cloves, and crushed peppers. Bring to a rolling boil over high heat. Decrease the heat to medium and simmer, stirring often, for about 30 minutes, until the mixture is thick and spreads easily. Allow to cool and then refrigerate until completely chilled. Covered and refrigerated, the catsup will keep for 2 to 3 weeks.

CORN AND CHAYOTE RELISH ||| Called *chayotli* by the Aztec of Mexico, this

small, pear-shaped squash was one of their staple foods. The Maya favored the new, young flowering tendrils and made use of the roots. Some varieties of chayote have smooth skin while others have small curled spines. Other regional names for chayote are *christophene* and *mirliton.* This relish is wonderful with tacos or savory fry breads.

||| MAKES ABOUT 4 CUPS

1 small poblano chile

2 cups fresh corn kernels (2 ears)

1 chayote squash, with seed, cut into ¼-inch dice

1 jalapeño chile, seeded and minced

½ small red bell pepper, minced

¼ cup coarsely chopped cilantro

½ small red onion, finely chopped

¼ cup olive oil

Juice of 2 limes

¼ teaspoon sea or kosher salt

Pinch of freshly ground black pepper

Place the poblano chile directly over a flame or on a grill and cook, turning as needed, for 3 to 5 minutes, until the skin is charred. Place the chile in a plastic bag to steam for 5 minutes. When cool enough to handle, peel and seed the chile and cut into ¼-inch dice.

Combine the poblano chile, corn, squash, jalapeño chile, bell pepper, cilantro, and onion in a bowl. Add the oil and lime juice and mix well. Season with salt and pepper and let stand at room temperature for 30 minutes before serving. Covered and refrigerated, the relish will keep for about 2 days, but is best when served within a couple hours of preparation.

CHAYOTE SALAD ||| This versatile pear squash, also known as *mirliton*, has a multitude of uses, both cooked and raw, which include this refreshing salad. Serve this as a course preceding any of the braised meat dishes in this book. Also enjoy this salad with enchiladas, Hallacas (page 22), or tamales. ||| SERVES 4

1 orange, peeled, seeded, and segmented

2 chayotes, including the seed, coarsely grated

1/2 red onion, thinly sliced

1/4 cup loosely packed mint leaves, minced

2 tablespoons peanut oil

Juice of 1 lemon

Juice of 1 lime

Pinch of sea or kosher salt

Pinch of freshly ground black pepper

Combine all of the ingredients in a bowl and toss well to combine. Serve immediately.

WILD GINGER DIPPING SAUCE ||| This is an unusual and delectable dipping sauce for Wild Rice and Corn Fritters (page 14) or Clam and Cornmeal Fritters (page 18). Wild ginger occurs abundantly throughout the Pacific Northwest and can be found in farmers' markets in the region. ||| MAKES 1 CUP

1 cup mayonnaise

1 teaspoon minced fresh wild or cultivated ginger, or 1/2 teaspoon ground ginger

1/2 teaspoon Dijon mustard

1 teaspoon minced fresh parsley

1 teaspoon minced fresh chives

1 teaspoon capers, drained and minced

1 tablespoon Pickled Red Onions, drained and minced (page 40)

1/2 teaspoon juice from Pickled Red Onions (page 40)

1/4 teaspoon sea or kosher salt

Combine all the ingredients in a bowl and mix well with a whisk. Cover and refrigerate for at least 30 minutes before serving to allow the flavors to develop. Covered and refrigerated, the sauce will keep for 2 to 3 days.

PICKLED SUNCHOKES

||| Jerusalem artichokes, also known as sunchokes, are indigenous to the eastern coast of North America and are related to the sunflower, which is native to Peru. Among the first foods introduced by Native people to the fledgling European communities of the New World, Jerusalem artichokes still find their way into many regional dishes. These pickles are very good with cooked and sliced potatoes dressed with nut oil, or use them in any recipes calling for pickles. ||| Photographed with Pickled Mushrooms, see page 38.

||| MAKES 1 QUART

4 cups Jerusalem artichokes, scrubbed and sliced into 1/2-inch pieces

About 4 cups distilled white vinegar

1/4 cup sea or kosher salt

2 teaspoons ground turmeric

1 pearl onion

1 whole small red dried chile

1/2 teaspoon mustard seed

1 bay leaf

1 whole clove

1/2 teaspoon black peppercorns

1/2 teaspoon allspice berries

1/3 cup honey

Place the artichokes in a tall glass or ceramic crock with about 2 cups of the vinegar, or just enough to cover. Add the salt and 1 1/2 teaspoons of the turmeric. Cover and refrigerate overnight.

Drain the artichokes and place in a large heatproof bowl. Add the onion and chile.

Using cheesecloth, make a spice bundle of the remaining 1/2 teaspoon turmeric, the mustard seed, bay leaf, clove, peppercorns, and allspice. Tie the cheesecloth and place in a pot with the remaining 2 cups vinegar. Bring to a boil over high heat. Decrease the heat to medium and simmer for about 15 minutes to extract the spice flavors. Add the honey, increase the heat to high, and return to a boil. Pour the liquid over the artichokes and allow to cool completely. Cover and cure in the refrigerator for 1 week before serving. Keeps well in the refrigerator for up to 3 weeks.

PICKLED MUSHROOMS

||| Like their early ancestors, American Indians often choose to dry all of their surplus mushrooms; however, pickling is one of the best options for preserving them. These pickled mushrooms provide a bright counterpoint to braised, pit-cooked, or grilled meats. A version of this recipe in Diana Kennedy's *The Art of Mexican Cooking* inspired Fernando to develop his own method. ||| **MAKES ABOUT 2 1/2 CUPS**

1 teaspoon dried Mexican oregano or marjoram

2 tablespoons corn oil

1/2 white onion, sliced

1 pound any wild or cultivated mushrooms, stemmed, used whole, or cut into 1/3-inch slices

3 sprigs thyme

3 bay leaves

3 cloves garlic

4 serrano chiles, halved lengthwise

1 cup apple cider vinegar

3/4 teaspoon sugar

Pinch of sea or kosher salt

Pinch of freshly ground black pepper

Heat a small sauté pan over medium heat. Add the oregano and cook, stirring constantly, for 5 to 7 minutes, until toasted.

Heat the oil in a large sauté pan over medium-high heat. Add the onion and cook for 2 to 3 minutes, until softened. Do not let the onion brown. Add the oregano, mushrooms, thyme, and bay leaves. Cover tightly and cook over medium-high heat for about 12 minutes, until the mushrooms begin to turn color and soften. Add the garlic and chiles and cook for 3 minutes. Add the vinegar, sugar, salt, and pepper. Bring to a boil for 2 minutes. Remove from the heat and allow to cool completely. Cover and refrigerate for 2 to 3 days before serving. Bring the mushrooms to room temperature before serving. Store covered in the refrigerator for 2 to 3 months.

PICKLED RED ONIONS ||| These delicious onions are served by present-day Maya

throughout Mexico's Yucatán Peninsula and beyond. They can accompany Yucatán-Style Pork (page 89). The brine

adds a unique flavor to vinaigrettes or sauces. ||| Photographed with Pickled Mushrooms, see page 38. |||

MAKES ABOUT 1 CUP

1 teaspoon corn oil

1 red onion, thinly sliced

½ cup apple cider vinegar

Juice of 1 orange

Juice of 1 lime

Pinch of sea or kosher salt

Pinch of freshly ground black pepper

Place a nonreactive pan over medium-high heat and add the oil. Add the onion and cook for 5 to 7 minutes, until slightly wilted. Do not let the onion brown. Add the vinegar, orange juice, lime juice, salt, and pepper and bring to a boil for 1 to 2 minutes. Immediately transfer the onions with the liquid to a glass bowl or glazed ceramic crock. Place an inverted plate over the top to completely submerge the onions. Cover and refrigerate for at least 4 hours. These pickles last for several days in the refrigerator and are best served at room temperature.

TINY TOMATO NASTURTIUM PICKLES ||| The originator of these deli-

cious pickles is unknown, but this combination of two American native foods is always superb. The domesticated ver-

sion of the wild Mexican currant tomato is preferred, although any small variety produces good results. Nasturtiums

grow abundantly in many parts of the Western Hemisphere. You can gather young shoots or seed pods yourself, or buy

them at specialty grocers. ||| MAKES 2 CUPS

1 cup red currant tomatoes

1 cup yellow currant tomatoes

10 nasturtium shoots or seed pods

⅛ teaspoon sea or kosher salt

1 cup apple cider vinegar

Place the red and yellow currant tomatoes, nasturtium shoots, and salt in a clean jar. Place the vinegar in a saucepan and bring to a boil over high heat. Pour the vinegar over the tomatoes. Allow to cool completely, cover, and refrigerate for about 2 weeks to develop the flavors before serving. Store covered in the refrigerator for 2 to 3 months.

PICKLED MANGOES ||| This recipe produces wonderful pickles that are essential for a traditional luau as well as an appetizing accompaniment to any Hawaiian menu. Leaving the outer shell of the seed attached to the fruit gives the pickles a nice texture. These pickles are often cured with red food coloring; if you prefer a colored pickle, try adding dried hibiscus flowers, which infuses them with a natural rosy color and more flavor.

||| MAKES ABOUT 4 CUPS

2 unripe mangoes

1 cup packed brown sugar

3 tablespoons Hawaiian, sea, or kosher salt

1 1/2 cups water

1/2 cup distilled white vinegar

6 dried hibiscus flowers (optional)

Peel the mangoes with a paring knife and cut in half lengthwise through the seed. Remove the core or kernel of the seed, leaving the fruit attached to the outer shell. Cut the fruit into 1-inch slices. Place the slices in a jar, glass bowl, or glazed crock.

To prepare the brine, combine the sugar, salt, water, vinegar, and hibiscus flowers in a saucepan over high heat and bring to a boil. Stir often to dissolve the sugar and salt. Remove the brine from the heat and allow to cool to room temperature.

Pour the brine over the mango slices, cover, and refrigerate. Cure for 3 to 4 days, turning the pickles from time to time in the brine to steep them evenly. Covered and refrigerated, the mangoes will keep for 2 to 3 months.

GUATEMALAN POTATO AND FRESH GREEN BEAN SALAD

||| This is a typical Maya recipe that has changed little (save in the use of modern appliances) over time. The ageless flavors of pumpkin seeds, tomatillos, potatoes, and beans meld seamlessly and produce a nutritionally balanced and delicious salad. As an alternative to the chilled salad, try serving it warm, wrapped in a fresh tortilla with a little crumbled cheese, or serve it over steamed rice for a satisfying meatless meal. ||| SERVES 5 TO 6

1 pound small new potatoes, quartered

1 teaspoon sea or kosher salt

2 3/4 cups green beans, stemmed and cut into bite-sized lengths

1 cup pumpkin or squash seeds

2 to 3 tomatillos, husked

2 cloves garlic

Pinch of freshly ground black pepper

Preheat the oven to 350° F.

Place the potatoes and salt in a saucepan with enough water to cover. Cook over medium-high heat for 12 to 15 minutes, until the potatoes are fork-tender. Remove with a slotted spoon and reserve the water. Allow the potatoes to cool completely. Return the water to a boil over medium-high heat. Add the beans and cook just until the water resumes a mild simmer. Remove with a slotted spoon and reserve the water. Cool the beans quickly in an ice water bath or place on a plate in the refrigerator for a rapid cool-down.

Spread the pumpkin seeds on a baking sheet and place in the oven. Toast for about 10 minutes, until lightly browned. Remove from the oven and allow to cool.

Place the tomatillos and garlic in a dry cast-iron skillet over medium-high heat. Cook, stirring often, for 5 to 7 minutes, until browned and softened.

Place the pumpkin seeds in a *molcajete* (a Mexican basalt mortar), food processor, or blender, and grind to a coarse paste. Add the tomatillos and garlic and process until smooth. Gradually add 2 to 2 1/2 cups of the reserved cooking water to make a dressing thick enough to generously coat the potatoes and beans.

To assemble the salad, place the potatoes and beans in bowl and sprinkle them with the black pepper. Add the dressing and toss to coat evenly. Serve immediately.

CHILEAN-STYLE AVOCADO AND SHRIMP SALAD |||

This classic New World salad seems as contemporary today as it must have been when it was first developed. Regional cooks throughout the Americas have added their own personal touch and, while the addition of mayonnaise is purely European, this combination is now an American tradition. ||| SERVES 4

2 cups water

1 bay leaf

$^1/_2$ teaspoon ground allspice

$^1/_2$ lemon, quartered

$^1/_2$ teaspoon sea or kosher salt

8 shrimp (16 to 20 count), peeled, deveined, and heads removed

SHRIMP SAUCE
1 anchovy fillet, soaked in a little milk to remove some of the salt

$^1/_2$ teaspoon minced flat-leaf parsley

$^1/_3$ cup mayonnaise

$^1/_2$ lemon

Pinch of freshly ground black pepper

Pinch of crushed red peppers

SALAD
2 ripe avocados

1 cup shredded green cabbage

Combine the water, bay leaf, allspice, lemon, and salt in a saucepan over high heat. Bring to a boil, then decrease the heat to medium-low and add the shrimp. Cook for 7 to 10 minutes, until the shrimp are curled and pink. Do not to overcook the shrimp, as they are significantly better if just cooked through. Drain the shrimp and allow to cool completely before assembling the salad.

To prepare the sauce, rinse the anchovy fillet, pat dry with paper towels, and mince. Combine the anchovy, parsley, and mayonnaise in a bowl. Place a strainer over the bowl and juice the lemon over the contents. Add the pepper and red peppers and whisk to blend completely.

To assemble the salad, cut the avocados in half lengthwise and remove the pits. With a large spoon, scoop out the avocado flesh and reserve the empty shell to present the salad. Distribute the cabbage among 4 salad plates. Make a hollow in the center of the cabbage and place the empty avocado shell in the hollow. Cut the avocado flesh into $^1/_2$-inch cubes. Place the shrimp and avocado in a bowl. Fold the sauce into the shrimp mixture and mound the salad in the avocado shells. Serve immediately.

≋ OPPOSITE: A young Mapuche woman from the Temuco region of Chile with a basket used for carrying vegetables. (P09653)

TOMATILLO AND PUMPKIN SEED VINAIGRETTE |||

In Mexico, *El Día de los Muertos* (The Day of the Dead) is celebrated on November 2. On that day, the dead are believed to return to the earth to visit the living. Frank Mendez, a fabulous Mexican-American cook, helped develop this recipe for a special Day of the Dead menu. It is terrific on most salad greens, with toasted pumpkin seeds sprinkled over the salad as a crunchy counterpoint. ||| MAKES ABOUT 2 CUPS

¼ cup pumpkin seeds

6 to 8 tomatillos (about ½ pound), husked

½ cup corn oil

½ cup rice vinegar or mild vinegar

½ tablespoon apple cider vinegar

¼ teaspoon sea or kosher salt

Pinch of cayenne pepper

Preheat the oven to 350°F. Spread the pumpkin seeds on a baking sheet and place in the oven. Toast for about 10 minutes, until lightly browned. Remove from the oven and allow to cool. Finely chop the pumpkin seeds.

Place the tomatillos in a saucepan with enough water to cover and bring to a boil. Cook for about 5 minutes, until softened and cooked through. Drain and allow the tomatillos to cool completely. Place the pumpkin seeds and tomatillos in a *molcajete* (a Mexican basalt mortar), food processor, or blender and process to a coarse paste. Transfer the paste to a bowl. Using a whisk, incorporate the oil and then the rice vinegar and apple cider vinegar into the mixture. Season with the salt and cayenne pepper. Cover and refrigerate for about 1 hour before serving to allow the flavors to develop.

WILD FLOWER HONEY VINAIGRETTE ||| This simple dressing is particularly good when tossed with Bibb lettuces and sliced apples or ripe pears. It tends to draw out the flavors when drizzled over ripe melon. Try brushing it on chicken or a mild fish, such as trout or lake perch, as a marinade a few hours before cooking. It also makes a luscious glaze. ||| MAKES ABOUT 1 CUP

2 tablespoons wild flower honey

½ cup corn or sunflower oil

¼ cup apple cider vinegar

Combine all of the ingredients in a bowl and mix well with a whisk. This vinaigrette should be used soon after preparing.

CREAMY MEXICAN HERB DRESSING ||| This dressing is an excellent

dip for fresh raw vegetables and is equally delicious served over crunchy romaine or crisp new leaf lettuces.

||| MAKES ABOUT 2¹/₄ CUPS

1¹/₂ tablespoons pumpkin or squash seeds

¹/₄ cup coarsely chopped cilantro

¹/₂ bunch fresh basil leaves

2 tomatillos, husked

2 cloves garlic, minced

Juice of 1 lime

1¹/₂ tablespoons corn oil

Pinch of sea or kosher salt

Pinch of freshly ground black pepper

¹/₄ cup buttermilk

³/₄ cup sour cream

Preheat the oven to 350°F. Spread the pumpkin seeds on a baking sheet and place in the oven. Toast for about 10 minutes, until lightly browned. Remove from the oven and allow to cool.

Place the pumpkin seeds, cilantro, basil, tomatillos, garlic, lime juice, oil, salt, pepper, and buttermilk in a food processor or blender and process until smooth. Transfer to a bowl and whisk in the sour cream to form a thick, creamy dressing. Covered and refrigerated, the dressing will keep for 2 to 3 days.

BERRY VINEGAR ||| Do not use homemade vinegar or wine vinegar to make berry vinegar.

The mother, a membrane made of yeast and bacterial cells that develops on the surface, will impair the process.

||| MAKES 1 CUP

¹/₄ cup raspberries, strawberries, huckleberries, or elderberries

1 cup distilled white vinegar or apple cider vinegar

Place the berries and vinegar in a glass jar with a tight-fitting lid. Cover and seal tightly. Place in the refrigerator for 3 weeks or more to steep. Strain and discard the berries before using the vinegar. This vinegar keeps for months in the refrigerator.

For a quicker method (but less pronounced flavors), place the berries and vinegar in a stainless-steel saucepan and bring to a simmer over high heat. Immediately remove the pan from the heat and steep for a minimum of 4 hours. Allow to cool completely, then strain and discard the berries before using the vinegar. This vinegar also keeps for months in the refrigerator.

BERRY VINAIGRETTE |||

The use of refined oils with flavored vinegar may have originated centuries ago with the early peoples of the Americas, who combined fruits, nuts, and greens. The possibilities are abundant for this vivid dressing, which incorporates vinegar flavored with your favorite berry. ||| Combine fresh, aggressive greens, such as dandelion, lambs-quarters, or watercress, with sweet lettuces for a balanced salad. The addition of fresh berries, dried fruits, and toasted nuts provides texture and flavor. For a more substantial salad, serve with pine nuts and a warm piece of fresh sheep's milk cheese. (Sheep products and pine nuts are two of the American Southwest's oldest tribal staples.) Toss the salad with enough of the dressing to coat the leaves thoroughly. Warm Grill Bread (page 150) or Cornmeal Crackers (page 162) complement salads made with this vinaigrette. ||| MAKES 2¼ CUPS

½ cup berry vinegar (page 47)

1¾ cups hazelnut or walnut oil

¼ teaspoon sea or kosher salt

Pinch of freshly ground black pepper

Combine all the ingredients in a bottle with a tight-fitting lid. Shake vigorously to incorporate the oil into the vinegar. If you like an emulsified dressing, place the ingredients in a blender and process on the highest setting until completely combined. Store unused vinaigrette in a tightly covered container for up to 1 week.

BALSAMIC-BERRY VINAIGRETTE: Add 2 tablespoons of aged balsamic vinegar to round out and accentuate the berry flavor.

LEMON-BERRY VINAIGRETTE: Add the juice of half a lemon to brighten and provide balance to the vinaigrette.

HAZELNUT VINAIGRETTE ||| Use this vinaigrette to dress blanched fresh fiddlehead

ferns or asparagus. The nut oil and citrus seem to have a particular affinity for the aggressively flavored tendrils of

young ferns. A few wood sorrel leaves, cooked wild rice, and some toasted hazelnuts are also good additions to the mix.

||| MAKES ABOUT 2¹/₄ CUPS

½ cup rice or mild vinegar

½ cup hazelnut oil

1 cup corn or sunflower oil

1 tablespoon freshly squeezed lemon juice

1 tablespoon freshly squeezed lime juice

1 tablespoon freshly squeezed grapefruit
  juice

Combine all of the ingredients in a bottle with a tight-fitting lid. Shake vigorously to incorporate the oils into the vinegar. This vinaigrette should be used soon after preparing.

MAPLE VINAIGRETTE ||| The resonant flavor of maple syrup comes through clearly,

although only two tablespoons are needed to make this tasty dressing. Use this vinaigrette with a mix of lettuces, both

bitter and mild, tossed with sliced apples or pears and toasted pine nuts or hazelnuts. ||| MAKES ABOUT 2¹/₃ CUPS

½ cup applesauce

1 cup sunflower, corn, or peanut oil

¾ cup apple cider vinegar

2 tablespoons pure maple syrup

Combine all of the ingredients in a bottle with a tight-fitting lid. Shake vigorously to incorporate the oils into the vinegar. Covered and refrigerated, this vinaigrette will keep for up to 1 week.

CHAPTER THREE

SOUPS

≋ Sioux carved horn double-handled spoon. South Dakota. (T9068)

Whether for the chowders prepared by the Abenaki of present-day Maine or for the delicious stews of the Peruvian Quechua, methods of boiling and simmering have been used by Native people for millennia. The ingredients were as diverse thousands of years ago as they are now: roots, vegetables, meats, fowl, nuts, berries, fruits, grasses, grains, herbs, and spices all were incorporated into nutritious soups. Coastal people and those living near lakes and streams relied on foods such as seaweed, kelp, cattails, and wapato to use in soups and stews as the main ingredient, or to flavor and accompany fish, shellfish, or waterfowl.

The potato, either fresh or dried, has been a common ingredient in soups and stews, due in no small part to Inka contributions to agronomy and mastery of the technique of freeze-drying. Pumpkin and squash play nearly as significant a role in many cultures and are easy to work with, particularly when preparing for groups or festive occasions.

Versions of soups made of duck, geese, and other waterfowl are found throughout the Americas. Modern chowders of North America, the equivalent of South America's *chupes*, are incarnations of very early fish and shellfish soups, the ingredients and preparations of which have evolved through cultural diversification. The Aleutian-style chowder in this chapter draws on the Russian influences that linger in Alaska.

ROAST PUMPKIN SOUP ||| Pumpkins, gourds, and squashes are among the oldest culti-

vated crops throughout the Americas. A form of pumpkin soup has long been made from Argentina to Ottawa. This modern recipe takes advantage of contemporary flavorings and produces a full-flavored soup. For a richer soup, try spooning on a dollop of crema (page 209) just before serving. The addition of lightly salted and toasted pumpkin seeds adds interesting texture and flavor to the soup. For a complete meal, steam Fresh Corn Dumplings (page 156) in the soup and serve with Chayote Salad (page 36). ||| SERVES 6 TO 8

1 (10-pound) pumpkin, stemmed, seeded, and cut into several wedges

1/4 cup corn oil

2 carrots, peeled and quartered

2 onions, sliced

1 celery stalk, coarsely chopped

1 tablespoon coriander seed

1 teaspoon black peppercorns

8 whole cloves

1/2 teaspoon ground cinnamon

3 to 4 cups chicken white stock (page 209) or water

2 tablespoons sherry vinegar (optional)

1 teaspoon Worcestershire sauce

1/8 teaspoon cayenne pepper

Sea or kosher salt

Preheat the oven to 375°F.

Lightly oil the pumpkin wedges and place in a roasting pan. In a bowl, toss the carrots, onions, and celery with the remaining oil to apply a thin coat. Spoon the vegetables into the roasting pan with the pumpkin. Bake for about 25 minutes, until the pumpkin and vegetables are easily pierced with a fork and cooked throughout. Remove from the oven and allow to cool.

Combine the coriander seed, peppercorns, and cloves in a spice mill and grind until fine. Combine the ground spices and cinnamon in a dry sauté pan and toast over medium heat for 5 to 7 minutes, until a pleasant aroma is released from the spices. Do not burn or overcook.

Scoop the pumpkin flesh into a bowl and discard the skin. In a food processor or blender, purée the pumpkin in batches, transferring the purée to a heavy saucepan over low heat. Purée the roasted vegetables and add to the pumpkin purée. Add enough stock to thin the purée to the consistency of heavy cream. Add the ground spices and increase the heat to medium-high. Bring the soup to a boil and then immediately decrease the heat to medium-low and simmer for 12 to 15 minutes. Add the vinegar, Worcestershire sauce, cayenne, and salt to taste. Ladle into soup bowls and serve immediately.

DUCK SOUP |||

Duck figures in the mix of seasonal foods for millions of Native peoples from North to South America. In most locales, there are two seasons for duck and other waterfowl due to their semiannual migrations. This adaptation was inspired by traditional recipes from Northwest tribes and by a version in *Jeremiah Tower's New American Classics.* It is practical in that the prime meat of the duck can be consumed first, leaving the bones and offal for this tasty soup. Serve with Buckskin Cakes (page 159). Bee balm can be found at specialty grocers. ||| SERVES 4

2 duck legs, skinned

2 duck thighs, skinned

1 duck heart

1 duck gizzard

1 (3-inch) piece wild ginger, or 1 (¼-inch) slice cultivated ginger, peeled

8 green onions, white parts thinly sliced, green parts cut into 2-inch lengths

6 cups duck or chicken brown stock (page 208)

Pinch of sea or kosher salt

Pinch of freshly ground black pepper

1 tomato, peeled and diced

1 tablespoon bee balm, cut into fine ribbons (optional)

2 sprigs cilantro, stemmed and coarsely chopped

2 basil leaves, cut into fine ribbons

Combine the legs, thighs, heart, gizzard, ginger, green onion whites, and duck stock in a pot over medium-high heat. Bring just to a simmer and, without boiling, cook for about 15 minutes. Using a slotted spoon, remove and discard the ginger. Simmer the soup gently for 25 to 35 minutes longer, until the meat is very tender and yields easily when pierced with a fork. Skim the surface of the soup with a spoon as foam accumulates. Remove the legs, thighs, heart, and gizzard with a slotted spoon and allow to cool slightly. Pull the meat from the leg and thigh bones and thinly slice all the meat, removing any small pieces of cartilage. Return the meat to the soup and simmer for 5 minutes, until warmed through. Taste the soup and add salt and pepper as necessary.

To serve, distribute the tomato in the bottom of 4 soup plates. Ladle the soup over the tomato. Sprinkle the green onion tops, bee balm, cilantro, and basil over the soup and serve immediately.

≈ A Haida ladle made of carved mountain sheep horn, with the handle representing the Raven. Queen Charlotte Islands, British Columbia. (6/9695)

ARGENTINE BEEF AND POTATO SOUP ||| Regional variations abound

for this simply delicious soup that is prevalent throughout the Western Hemisphere. This recipe was adapted from
Elisabeth Lambert Ortiz's *The Book of Latin American Cooking.* For a complete meal, serve this soup with Wild Mustard
Seed and Allium Crackers (page 163) and a leafy green salad. ||| SERVES 4

3/4 pound beef brisket or shoulder

4 cups beef brown stock (page 208) or
    canned low-sodium beef stock

1 1/2 tablespoons corn oil

2 teaspoons minced white onion

2 teaspoons minced red bell pepper

4 small new potatoes, cut into 6 wedges each

Pinch of cayenne pepper

Sea or kosher salt

Freshly ground black pepper

1 1/2 tablespoons minced fresh flat-leaf
    parsley, for garnish

Place the meat and 2 cups of the stock in a saucepan over medium-high heat. Bring to a boil, then decrease the heat to medium-low to achieve a gentle simmer. Cook for 2 hours, until very tender, adding water as necessary to keep the meat covered during cooking. With a slotted spoon, skim off the impurities as they accumulate. Transfer the meat to a cutting board and shred or cut into 1/2-inch cubes. Reserve the cooking liquid.

Heat a saucepan over medium-high heat and add the oil. Add the meat and cook for 10 to 12 minutes, until browned evenly on all sides. Add the onion and bell pepper, and cook, stirring often, for 3 to 5 minutes, without browning. Add the reserved cooking liquid, the remaining 2 cups stock, potatoes, and cayenne. Bring to a boil and immediately turn the heat down to medium-low. Cover and simmer for about 15 minutes, until the potatoes are tender. Season with salt, pepper, and cayenne to taste. Ladle into soup bowls, sprinkle with the parsley, and serve immediately.

Going Home with Koyah and Misho

WAKES, WHIPPOORWILLS, AND *DOM NA BO*

WHEN I WAS A GIRL in the 1950s, my little sister (we called her Peter) and I used to go to the reservation with our maternal grandparents, Koyah and Misho. It's on Highway 75, about thirty miles north of Topeka, where I grew up. Koyah and Misho grew up on the Prairie Band Potawatomi reservation and moved to Topeka in the early 1900s to find work. They often went back to visit, and I sometimes went along. Before we left for the drive north, Misho would load provisions into the trunk of the old Buick. We always took blankets, sugar, cans of coffee, cakes or pies, and toilet paper, and sometimes we took meat. In the 1950s, before the casino, there were no paved roads on the rez. It was a dusty ride on narrow dirt roads past corn and hay fields, stands of timber, and old houses with old cars parked out front.

≈ Marty Kreipe de Montaño and her grandmother, Lenora Blandin Bourdon (a.k.a. Koyah), in Topeka, Kansas, 1975.

I didn't realize it then, but we often went to the wakes and funerals of relatives and friends of my grandparents. I never asked questions about these events—it was just how things were with my grandparents. I can still see it. We arrive at the house where the body is laid out. People are sitting in all manner of chairs outside and inside the house. The smell of hardwood fires mixed with tobacco drifts on the air. Most folks talk softly in Potawatomi. The language is beautiful and has a wonderful soft sound. The words flow in a way that soothes the mind. Almost everyone chuckles as they talk. Making little jokes is part of the way of the people; maybe it's embedded in the language.

Plump old ladies with round faces, dressed in homemade cotton skirts and blouses, their long braids covered with scarves, are cooking *dom na bo* (corn soup) over fires in big black kettles set between two poles. When we contribute our meat, it is added to the pot, and the desserts and coffee are gratefully accepted and laid out on a table inside the house. A huge tin pot of boiling water on the stove is made into coffee. Some elderly women sit in rocking chairs, smoking tobacco in small corncob pipes.

Koyah and Misho talk to everyone in turn, moving from group to group. We follow along, listening to the sounds of the language. Sometimes they look at us, no doubt remarking on how we have grown, smiling if we are quiet and good and joking if we are loud or fidgety.

When we eat, we are given bowls of dom na bo accompanied by big pillows of delicious fluffy fry bread, and then we follow this with homemade pie. Later in the evening, when it cools off, we sit outside next to Koyah and Misho, on blankets cushioned by a low mound of straw. In the distance I hear the eerie cry of whippoorwills. I feel sleepy, as mourning songs in Potawatomi from inside the house rise and fall on the night air. The songs are preparing the living to let the departed go. My sister and I lie down on the blanket and Koyah covers us. We fall asleep, secure and full under the stars.

—Marty Kreipe de Montaño

Marty Kreipe de Montaño (Prairie Band Potawatomi) is the manager of the National Museum of the American Indian's resource centers. She has an M.A. in the ethnohistory of North American Indians from the University of Kansas. She is the co-author (with Arlene Hirschfelder) of an award-winning reference book, *The Native American Almanac.* **Her children's book,** *Coyote in Love with a Star,* **has received a design award for the illustrations by Tom Coffin. She also wrote** *Harvest Ceremony* **(with Jennifer Fell Hayes), a play produced by the NMAI. She has taught Native American history at New York University and has worked in museums for twenty years.**

PHOTO COURTESY OF MARTY KREIPE DE MONTAÑO

≈ Lenora Blandin Bourdon (Prairie Band Potawatomi), 1889–1991. In this picture, she is standing on the steps of Kiva Hall at Haskell Institute, U.S. Indian Training School (now Haskell Indian Nations University), circa 1913.

ALEUTIAN-STYLE DUNGENESS CRAB AND SCALLOP
CHOWDER |||

In the late eighteenth century, Russians became the first non-Native people to settle in what is now Alaska. Their culinary heritage continues to influence many Alaskan tribes, including the Aleuts. This type of chowder is among the earliest forms of soup and it continues to be made throughout the Americas. Cream was used only after European contact. ||| Be sure to poach the scallops until they are just barely cooked through, as they will be hopelessly dry if overcooked. The crab need only be heated because it is already cooked. Adding the herbs just before serving will give the chowder its distinctly fresh flavor. Serve with Buckskin Cakes (page 159) and honey for a light lunch, accompanied by a crisp salad. ||| Chicken stock is a good alternative to clam juice or fish stock for those folks who are squeamish about strong fish flavors. But if a resonant shellfish and fish flavor is your desire, by all means use that stock. ||| SERVES 4 AS A LIGHT MEAL OR 6 AS A STARTER

1 tablespoon corn or sunflower oil

1 bacon slice, chopped

6 cups chicken white stock (page 209)
  or clam juice

1 cup water

1 leek, white part only, sliced

1/2 small white onion, diced

8 to 10 small new potatoes, quartered

12 ounces sea scallops, side muscle or foot
  removed

1 1/2 cups heavy cream

1 cooked Dungeness crab, shelled, or
  1/2 pound fresh crabmeat, picked over
  for shells

1 1/2 tablespoons fresh tarragon leaves

1 1/2 tablespoons minced fresh chives

Pinch of sea or kosher salt

Pinch of freshly ground black pepper

Place a soup pot over medium-high heat. Add the oil and bacon and cook for 5 to 7 minutes, until the bacon is crisp. Pour off most or all of the fat. Add the stock, water, leek, onion, and potatoes. Bring to a boil, and then decrease the heat to medium-low. Simmer for 15 to 20 minutes, until the potatoes are fork-tender. Add the scallops and cook for 5 to 6 minutes, until the scallops are opaque and cooked through. Add the cream, crabmeat, tarragon, and chives. Taste for seasoning. (If using store-bought chicken stock, the bacon and crab will generally give over enough salt to flavor the chowder. If not, add salt and pepper to taste.) Cook for 2 to 3 minutes, until the crab is just heated through. Ladle into warm soup bowls and serve immediately.

CHOWDER WITH FRESH CORN: When in season, corn is a wonderful complement to the seafood. Add 1 1/2 cups fresh corn kernels when adding the scallops to the pan.

CLAM AND MUSSEL CHOWDER: Replace the scallops and crab with equal amounts of clams and mussels.

FISH CHOWDER: Replace the scallops and crab with equal amounts of fresh salmon, lingcod, or rockfish.

OYSTER AND SHRIMP CHOWDER: Replace the scallops and crab with equal amounts of oysters and fresh shrimp.

Northern Bean and Hominy Soup ||| As Native tribes were displaced by Europeans, they came into contact with previously distant groups. With this movement of people, trade items such as these white beans spread from the southern tip of South America to the American Southwest and ultimately throughout both continents. The combination of corn, from which hominy is derived, and beans is an American standard that continues to endure. ||| SERVES 4

2 cups northern beans

1 cup dried hominy, drained and rinsed

About 4 cups water or vegetable stock
(page 207)

3 to 4 ramps or green onions, white part
only, sliced

3 wild celery or domesticated celery stalks,
sliced

1 teaspoon sea or kosher salt

Place the beans in a bowl with water to cover and soak overnight.

Drain the beans and discard the water. Place the beans and dried hominy in a large saucepan and cover with the water. (If using canned hominy, add later, as directed.) Bring to a boil over high heat. Decrease the heat to medium-low and simmer for about 1 hour, stirring often and giving the pot a quarter-turn from time to time to avoid sticking. Using a slotted spoon, skim off the impurities as they accumulate. Add more water as necessary to keep the beans covered throughout cooking. If using canned hominy, add it now, along with the ramps, celery, and salt, and cook, stirring often, for 1 hour, or until the beans and hominy are tender. Ladle into warm bowls and serve immediately.

ASSINIBOINE-STYLE DUCK OR PHEASANT SOUP WITH NORTHERN BEANS AND HOMINY: Add ½ pound trimmed duck or pheasant thigh and leg meat and replace the water with duck or pheasant brown stock (page 208).

BEAN AND HOMINY SOUP WITH FRESH HERBS: Add ¼ cup minced fresh thyme, 2 minced garlic cloves, and 1 bay leaf for the last hour of cooking.

Fava Bean Soup with Mint

Thought to have originated in China or the Mediterranean, fava beans arrived through trade to the Americas and are right at home prepared in a manner similar to the native beans of the Americas. Adapted from a recipe in Diana Kennedy's *The Art of Mexican Cooking*, this is a rustic soup. It is prepared without meat, although you can make it with different meats and substitute their broth for the water. The soup is just right for a cool winter evening and the mint provides a fresh, bright counterpoint to the deeply flavored beans. Serve it with fresh tortillas and some wilted *qintoniles,* or greens—or with spinach dressed with fresh lime, salt, and olive oil. ||| SERVES 4

1/4 pound peeled dried fava beans

1 1/2 tablespoons olive oil, plus extra for drizzling

1/2 small white onion, coarsely chopped

1 to 2 cloves garlic, minced

2 peppercorns, cracked

1/8-inch piece canela

1 whole clove, crushed

About 1 1/2 quarts water

Generous pinch of sea or kosher salt

1 tomato, finely chopped

1 serrano chile, finely chopped

1 1/2 tablespoons minced fresh mint

2 tablespoons coarsely chopped cilantro

Place the fava beans in a colander and place the colander in a bowl. Fill the bowl with cool water and then pour off the water and leave the beans to drain over the bowl.

In a soup pot, heat 1 tablespoon of the oil over medium heat. Add the onion, garlic, peppercorns, canela stick, and clove. Cook, stirring, for 5 to 7 minutes, until the onion and garlic are soft but not brown. Add the fava beans and the water and bring to a boil. Decrease the heat to medium-low and simmer for about 1 hour, stirring often and giving the pot a quarter turn from time to time to avoid sticking. Add the salt and additional water if the soup seems too thick and continue to simmer.

Heat the remaining 1/2 tablespoon oil in a sauté pan over medium-high heat. Add the tomato and chile and cook, stirring continuously, for about 10 minutes, until the tomatoes have released their moisture and the mixture takes on a sauce-like appearance. Add the tomatoes, chile, mint, and two-thirds of the cilantro to the soup. Continue to cook, stirring often, for 35 to 40 minutes, until the soup has thickened and, although textured, melts on your palate.

To serve, ladle the soup into warm cups. Drizzle each cup with olive oil and sprinkle the remaining cilantro over the top.

Anasazi Bean and Hominy Soup

||| Many peoples throughout the American Southwest prepare a form of this bean soup. Pinto and tepary beans play as dominant a role as do Anasazi beans in the region, so you may prefer to use them. Actually, any bean may be substituted for the Anasazi beans, but keep in mind that every bean has a subtly different taste and texture. Hatch chiles are New Mexican green chiles that have a mild but delicious flavor. Serve this soup with warm blue corn tortillas or cornbread. ||| SERVES 4

2 cups dried Anasazi beans

About 6 cups water

2 cups dried hominy, drained and rinsed

1 teaspoon sea or kosher salt

1 tablespoon New Mexican chile powder, or another powdered chile

1 mild green Hatch or Anaheim chile

1/4 cup crumbled fresh sheep's or goat's milk cheese, for garnish (optional)

Place the beans in a bowl with water to cover and soak overnight.

Drain the beans and discard the water. Place the beans in a large saucepan. Add 4 cups of the water and bring to a boil over high heat. Using a slotted spoon, skim off the impurities as they accumulate. Decrease the heat to medium-low and simmer for about 1 hour, stirring often and adding water to keep the beans submerged. Add the hominy, salt, and chile powder. Cover the pot loosely and simmer for 1 to 2 hours, until the beans and hominy are tender. Stir often and continue to add enough water to keep the beans and hominy submerged.

Roast the chile over an open flame, on a grill, or under a broiler or fry it in a little oil, turning as needed for 2 to 3 minutes, until it is blistered and charred on all sides. Place the chile in a plastic bag for 5 minutes to steam. Peel the chile and remove the stem and seeds, then cut in half lengthwise, and cut into strips.

To serve, ladle the soup into warm bowls. Top each serving with a few of the roasted chile strips and some of the cheese. Serve immediately.

Hazelnut Soup

||| While nut soups are well established in the Northeast, hazelnuts continue to be a valued food to many other Native people across the United States and Canada. The Algonquin, Iroquois, and most other Native people of the northern woodlands regions prepared nuts in many ways, including versions of this delicious soup. Serve this with corn bread or, as one may do in the Northwest, with Buckskin Cakes (page 159). To make a richer tasting soup, add a dollop of crema (page 209) to each serving and top with a sprig of watercress and some additional toasted and chopped nuts. ||| SERVES 4

1 pound hazelnuts

6 to 8 ramps, green onions, or nodding onions, white part only

1/2 cup watercress, including tender stems

2 tablespoons hazelnut, sunflower, or corn oil

About 4 cups vegetable stock (page 207) or water

2 teaspoons sea or kosher salt

Preheat the oven to 350°F. Spread the hazelnuts on a baking sheet and place in the oven. Cook for 12 to 15 minutes, until toasted. Remove from the oven and allow to cool. When cool enough to handle, place the nuts in a kitchen towel and rub vigorously to remove as much of the papery skins as possible.

Trim the roots from the ramps and remove any woody stems and flowers. Thinly slice the ramps, with their tops on, and set aside. Rinse and drain the watercress, removing woody stems or pale leaves. Chop the watercress coarsely.

Heat the oil over medium heat in a large saucepan. Add the ramps and watercress and wilt for 3 to 5 minutes, stirring continuously. Add the stock and hazelnuts. Increase the heat to medium-high and bring to a boil. Decrease the heat to medium-low and simmer for about 30 minutes, until the nuts are softened and the flavors have developed. In small batches, transfer the soup to a food processor or blender and process until smooth (don't fill the processor more than one-third full). Return the purée to the saucepan and bring to a simmer over medium heat. Add more liquid to thin, if necessary, and stir in the salt. Ladle into warm bowls and serve immediately.

SUNFLOWER SEED SOUP: Substitute peeled and toasted sunflower seeds for the hazelnuts and skip the toasting step.

WALNUT SOUP: Substitute black walnuts for the hazelnuts.

WAPATO

BEFORE 1805 AND THE ARRIVAL of Lewis and Clark's exploration party, Sauvie Island in Oregon was known as Wapato Island to its original inhabitants, the Multnomah. They named it for the numerous wild potato-like plants that grew in the island's wetlands. Wapato at one time grew and flourished throughout much of the Americas in ponds, marshes, wetlands, and along riverbanks and streams. Although it is all but extinct in North America, the native plant, *Sagittaria latifolia,* can still be found growing wild on Sauvie Island.

When Lewis and Clark arrived on the island, the Multnomah people showed them immense hospitality. According to the explorers' journals, they were fed wapato and smelt, among other foods, and the expedition party traded with the Multnomah for the plant.

Sauvie Island lies fifteen miles northwest of downtown Portland, Oregon. It stands between three important waterways: the mighty Columbia River to the east, the Willamette River to the south, and the Multnomah Channel, a branch of the Willamette, to the west. Several lakes cover a portion of the interior. It is warm and generally dry in the summer, the fall is sporadically wet, and the winter sees abundant rain and colder weather. Spring also is wet. This weather lends itself to almost perfect conditions for growing and harvesting wapato.

The edible part of wapato is the root. This root, or solid tuber, is attached to a tall stalk with an arrowhead-shaped green leaf that can be spotted growing above the water. Because of the shape of the leaf, wapato is also called the arrowhead plant. Its taste is mild, like a russet potato, although it is a little starchier and has a distinct, nutty flavor.

The traditional way to harvest the bulb is to wade into the water barefoot and feel for the bulbs with your feet in the soft mud. When harvesting, you can either use a stick or your toes to pry the bulbs from the floor of the pond. Once you feel the bulb you dig under it to dislodge it, and it pops to the top of the water. You then break off the bulb from the stalk and keep the bulb.

A traditional way to prepare the tuber is to cook it in a pit fire until it is soft and unctuous. It is also frequently added to soups or stews. This traditional use continues today at potlatches and spring root celebrations.

PHOTO BY MARLENE DIVINA

≈ Fernando Divina, second from right, with friends after a day of harvesting wapato.

SALMON SOUP WITH WAPATO AND CATTAIL SHOOTS

||| Cattail, *Typha latifolia,* was once one of the Western Hemisphere's most important plants. It was used by many tribes throughout the Americas not only as a source of food but also to make a variety of weavings, including baskets, mats, and rugs. The silky down was used to stuff bedding, and at least several Plains tribes used the fluffy tops as padding for baby diapers. Many tribes residing along the Columbia and Willamette rivers in Washington and Oregon prepared a version of this soup. ||| You are likely to find all of the ingredients for this soup in the same location in the wild. Cattails are sometimes available in farmers' markets in the Northwest, or you can order them by mail (see sources, page 215). ||| SERVES 4 TO 6

12 wapato roots or waxy new potatoes, peeled and cut into 1-inch pieces

6 to 8 (4- to 6-inch) cattail shoots or fresh hearts of palm, trimmed of woody exterior and sliced

6 green onions, or 8 to 10 nodding onions, white part only, sliced

4 cups water or vegetable stock (page 207)

5 juniper berries

1 pound fresh salmon steak

Pinch of sea or kosher salt

Place the wapato, cattails, onions, water, and juniper berries in a large saucepan and bring to a boil over high heat. Decrease the heat to medium and simmer for about 15 minutes, until the wapato is tender. Add the salmon and salt and cook for 8 to 10 minutes, until the salmon is just underdone. Remove the salmon with a slotted spoon or a spatula and continue simmering the soup.

Place the salmon on a clean work surface and gently remove the skin with the tines of a fork. Lift the central and belly bones away from the flesh and pull away the belly membrane.

To serve, break the salmon into bite-sized pieces and evenly distribute the meat among warm soup bowls. With a slotted spoon, evenly distribute the vegetables into the bowls. Ladle the broth over, and serve immediately.

≈ Elaborately carved Haida wooden ladle. The ladle is carved with the Bear, Hawk, and Fish crests. (22/6301)

BUFFALO CHILI ‖

Inspired by a version in *Jeremiah Tower's New American Classics,* this chili sings the praises of contemporary Native America. For an extraordinary feast, spoon some uncooked Fresh Corn Dumplings (page 156) into the chili and cover tightly for the last 40 minutes of cooking, or serve the chili with warm tortillas (page 152) or Fry Bread or Grill Bread (page 150). Excellent garnishes include crumbled or grated cheese, a dollop of crema (page 209), and a generous spoonful of Fresh Mexican Tomato Salsa (page 30). Most red meats are suitable substitutes for the buffalo in this recipe, although more or less liquid may be needed to compensate for the fat content of the meat. ‖ SERVES 4

Pinch of cayenne pepper

½ teaspoon sweet paprika

1½ tablespoons ground poblano chile,
    or another type of ground chile

1 teaspoon crushed red peppers

1 bay leaf

1 tablespoon ground cumin

2 teaspoons dried Mexican oregano

2 tablespoons sunflower, corn,
    or safflower oil

2 to 3 pounds buffalo brisket or stew meat,
    trimmed and cut into 1-inch cubes

2 wild boar bacon or pork bacon slices,
    cut into ¼-inch cubes

½ white onion, minced

8 to 10 cloves garlic, minced

½ lemon, with rind, seeded and minced

½ lime, with rind, seeded and minced

About 3 cups brown stock (page 208)

3 tablespoons masa harina, or
    1 white corn tortilla, crumbled

1 tablespoon sea or kosher salt

½ teaspoon freshly ground black pepper

Combine the cayenne pepper, paprika, poblano chile, red peppers, bay leaf, cumin, and oregano in a dry sauté pan over medium-high heat. Carefully toast for 3 to 5 minutes, stirring constantly to prevent burning.

Heat a heavy saucepan over medium-high heat and add the oil. Add the buffalo and cook, turning with a fork, for 12 to 15 minutes, until browned on all sides. Add the bacon, onion, and garlic and cook, stirring often, for 5 minutes, until the onion is softened and translucent. Add the toasted spices, lemon, and lime and cook for 5 minutes, stirring often and rotating the pan on the heat to prevent burning or excessive sticking. Add 2 cups of the stock. Bring to a boil, stirring and rotating the pan frequently, and then decrease the heat to medium-low. Cover and simmer, stirring occasionally, for 30 to 40 minutes, until the meat is cooked but not quite fork-tender.

In a bowl, whisk the remaining 1 cup stock with the masa, salt, and pepper and stir into the chili. Be sure to fully incorporate the masa-stock mixture. Increase the heat to medium-high and bring the chili to a boil. Decrease the heat to low and simmer, stirring occasionally, for 30 minutes, until the meat is fork-tender. Skim the surface with a slotted spoon to remove any impurities as they accumulate and rotate the pan often. The chili should yield tender chunks of meat immersed in a rich, thick sauce. Adjust the liquid as needed. Serve warm.

VENISON CHILI: Substitute 2½ pounds of trimmed and cubed venison meat for the buffalo.

COLD AVOCADO SOUP COLOMBIA-STYLE ||| Avocados have more

vitamin E than any other fruit and, in addition to their high fat content, are fairly high in B vitamins. They are thought

to have originated in Central America, where they probably were cultivated as early as seven thousand years ago. The

avocado was grown some five thousand years ago in Mexico, and, according to legend, in 1519 Cortés found the fruit

flourishing in the region of present-day Mexico City. ||| SERVES 4

2 tablespoons avocado oil or corn oil

1 small white onion, finely chopped

1 small aji or serrano chile, seeded and
   minced

2 potatoes, peeled and cut into ½-inch dice

4 cups vegetable stock (page 207) or water

2 ripe avocados

1 cup crema (page 209) or whipped cream

2 tablespoons coarsely chopped cilantro,
   for garnish

Heat the oil in a heavy saucepan over medium-high heat. Add the onion and cook for 5 to 7 minutes, until soft. Do not let the onion brown. Add the chile and cook, stirring, for 3 to 5 minutes. Add the potatoes and stock and bring to a boil. Decrease the heat to low and simmer for about 20 minutes, until the potatoes are tender and easily pierced with a fork. Remove from the heat and allow to cool for 10 minutes.

In small batches, transfer the soup to a food processor or blender and process until smooth. Transfer the purée to a large bowl.

Peel and pit the avocados and spoon the flesh into the food processor. Add enough of the puréed soup to cover the avocados and process until smooth. Pour the avocado purée into the soup and use a wire whisk to fully incorporate. Cover the soup loosely with plastic wrap. Allow to cool completely at room temperature.

To serve, fold ³/₄ cup of the crema into the soup until fully incorporated. Ladle the soup into frozen or chilled bowls. Top with the remaining ¼ cup crema and divide the cilantro among the servings. Serve at once.

THREE SISTERS STEW |||

Many American Indians refer to squash, corn, and beans as the Three Sisters. The three plants grow well together. The bean climbs the natural trellis of the corn stalk, while the squash shades the ground below, discouraging other plants from spreading and choking the corn roots. Each plant also takes different nutrients from the soil. ||| Serve the stew with warm tortillas or with chochoyotes (page 19) or Fresh Corn Dumplings (page 156). The uncooked dumplings are added to the stew once it is brought to a boil. Cover the pot and place in a hot oven for 12 to 15 minutes, until the dumplings are cooked throughout, or cook on the stovetop over low heat. ||| SERVES 4

1 cup dried chestnut or Christmas lima beans, or any broad bean

2 Roma tomatoes, halved

1 poblano chile

1 tablespoon corn oil

1/2 small white onion, thinly sliced

1 summer squash, quartered and sliced 1/2 inch thick

1/2 pound fresh green or wax beans, stringed

Kernels from 2 ears fresh corn

2 tablespoons minced epazote or cilantro

1/4 cup salsa verde

1/4 cup salsa roja

2 cups vegetable stock (page 207) or water

Sea or kosher salt

Freshly ground black pepper

Place the dried beans in a saucepan and add water to cover. Cover, place over medium-high heat, and bring to a boil. Remove from the heat and let steep for 1 hour. Place over medium-high heat and bring to a boil. Decrease the heat to medium-low and cook for about 2 1/2 hours, until tender. Drain well.

Place the tomatoes and chile directly over a flame or on a grill and cook, turning as needed, for 3 to 5 minutes, until the skins are charred. Place the chile in a plastic bag to steam for 5 minutes. When cool enough to handle, peel and seed the tomatoes. Peel the chiles and cut in half lengthwise. Remove the stem and white membrane and scrape the seeds away and discard. Cut the chile into 6 pieces.

Heat the oil in a heavy saucepan over medium-high heat. Add the onion and cook, stirring often, for 5 to 7 minutes, until softened. Do not let the onion brown. Add the squash and cook, stirring continuously, for 1 minute, until softened. Add the dried beans, fresh beans, corn, epazote, salsa verde, salsa roja, and stock and bring to a boil. Decrease the heat to medium, add the tomatoes and chiles, and simmer for 5 minutes. Season with salt and pepper to taste. Serve in warm bowls, allowing 1 tomato half per person.

Chapter Four

Meats &
Wild Game

 Cheyenne woman scraping hide, circa 1902, Colony, Oklahoma. (N13597)

Over time, many American Indians made the transition from hunting and gathering to establishing agricultural communities. With the advent of farming technologies, great changes to the Native diet occurred, which can be traced over the centuries. When European animals were introduced, the Native American diet changed again. While the meats of wild deer, wild boar, wild turkey, buffalo, and other game are still consumed, the domesticated hybrid versions of these meats have become commonplace.

From the Maya in Central America to the Salish on the Northwest Coast, people of the Western Hemisphere, including Hawai'i, share the tradition of fire-pit cookery. Fire-pit cookery best exemplifies the joining of two elements: water (converted to steam) and fire. A pit is dug and lined with rock. A fire built in the pit is allowed to burn down to glowing embers. Plant or animal foods are wrapped, placed in the pit, and left to steam. The Maya of the Yucatán wrap wild boar or pork in banana leaves, while the Zapotec of Oaxaca encase their meats in the leaves of the century plant. The Tsimshian of the Northwest Coast favor ironwood leaves, ferns, and seaweed to impart flavor to their fish and waterfowl. In addition to banana leaves, Hawaiians use ti and taro leaves for wrapping the foods for their glorious luaus, as well as for everyday meals.

In the following recipes, freely substitute your favorite meats, and use what is easily available. With few exceptions, most kinds of meat fare well prepared according to the methods described.

BRAISED AMERICAN BUFFALO

||| Once officially listed among endangered species, American bison is now plentiful. Efforts by the U.S. and Canadian governments, and by Native breeding programs, have been successful in restoring the population. An indigenous cooperative, the InterTribal Bison Cooperative (ITBC), promulgates the breeding, ranching, and sale of buffalo (see sources, page 214). The sale of buffalo meat helps support this and other important programs designed to restore buffalo to its prominent role as a nutritious food. Buffalo is much leaner than beef and has higher nutritional value. ||| There was a time when the people of the Great Plains of the United States and Canada centered their lives around the buffalo. The animal supplied them with all their basic needs—food, clothing, and housing (tipis)—and was also used to make tools, musical instruments, and even children's toys. Through trade, buffalo had an impact even on those who lived on the fringes of its habitat. During the eighteenth century, the Pueblo community of Taos, northeast of Santa Fe, New Mexico, was the hub of an annual trade fair where Plains, Great Basin, Southwest, and Mexican tribes gathered. The influences of those tribes were incorporated into the lives of the Taos Indians and remain vibrant and visible today. The Taos Pueblo people host a great celebration and Buffalo Dance annually. ||| This recipe unites Shoshone and Taos Pueblo food styles, using modern materials and cooking methods. Buffalo may be obtained from your butcher by special order or from specialty food markets. Feel free to substitute your favorite foraged or cultivated root vegetable for the carrots to add a more traditional element to this satisfying dish. Wild mustard root, celery root, turnips, or parsnips make nice complements. Fresh Corn Dumplings (page 156) are a lovely addition. ||| SERVES 4 TO 6

≈ OPPOSITE: Detail from *The Exploits of Poor Wolf,* Hidatsa Second Chief, circa early 1900s. Artist unknown. "Poor Wolf kills a buffalo cow, and gives his entire equipment to the first man who comes to him, because his heart feels good." (T4/2446A)

1 Hatch chile or any mild green chile

2 tomatoes, halved

1 white onion, quartered

2 tablespoons corn oil

2 pounds buffalo shoulder or leg meat,
    trimmed and cut into 1-inch pieces

Sea or kosher salt

Freshly ground black pepper

Unbleached all-purpose flour, for dredging

1/4 cup canned tomato purée

2 cloves garlic, minced

2 carrots, peeled and sliced 1/2 inch thick

1/2 pound wild or cultivated mushrooms,
    cut into 1/2-inch slices

4 cups buffalo brown stock (page 208) or
    canned low-sodium beef stock

Prepare a hot fire in a charcoal grill or preheat a gas grill to high. Place the chile, tomatoes, and onion on the grill rack and cook, turning often, for 4 to 5 minutes, until the skins of the chile and tomatoes are slightly blackened and blistered and the onion is lightly browned and softened. Place the chile in a plastic bag for 5 minutes and let steam. Peel the tomatoes and cut into 1/2-inch cubes. Peel, stem, and seed the chile and cut into 1/2-inch dice.

Heat the oil in a large heavy saucepan over medium-high heat (for tips on braising, see page 203). Season the meat with salt and pepper and then roll in the flour, shaking gently to remove any excess. Add the meat to the pan and cook, turning, for 10 to 12 minutes, until evenly browned. Add the tomato purée, garlic, carrots, and mushrooms. Cook, stirring, for about 5 minutes, until the vegetables are softened but not browned. Add the stock and bring to a boil. Decrease the heat to medium-low, cover tightly, and simmer for about 1 hour. Alternatively, place in an oven preheated to 350°F and cook for about 1 hour. Add the grilled vegetables and continue braising the buffalo for 1 hour more, or until the meat yields easily when pierced with a fork. Serve immediately.

BRAISED BEEF: Substitute 2 pounds beef brisket for the buffalo.

BRAISED PORK: Substitute 2 pounds boneless country-style ribs for the buffalo.

"Poor Wolf" killing a buffalo cow, and gives his Entire Equipments to the first man who comes to him, because his heart feels good."

CHARQUI (JERKY) ||| It is no wonder that this ancient snack retains its popularity, bridging

all cultural boundaries. Dried meat is very satisfying and easy to prepare. Once you have mastered these simple steps,

experiment with flavorings that reflect your own taste. This recipe is an adaptation of one from E. Barrie Kavasch's excel-

lent book, *Enduring Harvests*. It was served during a presentation at a Slow Food International symposium in Turin, Italy,

where thousands of attendees were able to sample American bison for the first time. For tips on smoking foods, see

page 203. ||| MAKES 1 1/4 TO 1 1/2 POUNDS

5 pounds buffalo top round or
    beef top round

1/2 cup sea or kosher salt

1/2 cup pure maple syrup

1/2 cup ground or puréed wild or cultivated
    ginger, or 2 teaspoons ground ginger

1/2 cup ground or puréed wild or cultivated
    white onion, or 2 teaspoons onion
    powder

1/4 cup coarsely ground black pepper

Prepare a food dryer, smoker, oven, or grill, making certain there is no visible flame or that the setting is at its lowest. You will achieve good results in as few as 4 to 6 hours by using the lowest oven setting. Longer drying over lower heat provides deeper flavor and more pliant, supple dried meat.

To gain the best yield from this preparation, "seam" the top round. You may choose to have your butcher provide this service, attempt it yourself, or skip the entire procedure and simply cut the meat into manageable pieces. Top round has natural seams that are easily cut by lifting and separating one section from the other while slipping a sharp knife between them and cutting away the connective tissues or muscle fiber. Trim the tough membrane and any visible fat and cut the sections into approximately 1-pound pieces. Wrap the meat in plastic wrap and place in the freezer for 30 to 45 minutes, until partially frozen. This will help the slicing process. Don't freeze the meat solid or you will not be able to cut it.

Using a sharp knife, slice the partially frozen meat with the grain as thinly as possible. The meat should hold its shape and be manageable. If it is tearing or difficult to handle, it is sliced too thin. Cover the meat with plastic wrap and place in the freezer or refrigerator while preparing the flavorings.

Combine the salt, maple syrup, ginger, onion, and pepper in a bowl and whisk together or briskly stir with a wooden spoon. Pour the brine into a shallow pan large enough to hold the meat strips. Press each strip into the seasoning mixture. Without overlapping, lay the strips on drying racks, smoking racks, or a plastic- or parchment paper–lined baking sheet. Place the racks or pans of seasoned strips in the prepared dryer, smoker, oven, or on the grill, and cover. The maximum temperature should be 120°F to 150°F. The smoker, oven, or grill may take 6 to 8 hours, and the food dryer may take up to 24 hours. Check often; the strips should be well glazed and snap when bent. When they are ready, transfer to wire racks and allow to cool completely. Store tightly covered in a cool place for up to 3 months.

Sonoran-Style Beef Deshebrada

||| Sonora is a region located in the far north of Mexico. Cattle have become an important commodity here, and beef figures heavily in the diet of present-day Sonorans. Meat that is cooked and then shredded for filling is called deshebrada. This preparation is the basis for many dishes and has many uses, ranging from fillings for enchiladas, tacos, burritos, tamales (page 21), and omelet. It can also serve as a topping for Fry Bread (page 150). There are many versions of this dish, dictated by family tradition or by the ingredients at hand. ||| **MAKES ABOUT 2¹/₂ CUPS**

1 pound beef chuck or brisket, trimmed and cut into 3- to 4-inch pieces

¹/₂ small white onion, coarsely chopped

2 cloves garlic

1 bay leaf

1 teaspoon sea or kosher salt

About 2 cups brown stock (page 208) or water

¹/₈ teaspoon freshly ground black pepper

¹/₂ teaspoon dried Mexican oregano or marjoram

¹/₄ teaspoon dried basil leaves

1¹/₄ teaspoons sweet paprika

1 cup Fresh Mexican Tomato Salsa (page 30)

Place the meat in a heavy saucepan over high heat. Add the onion, garlic, bay leaf, salt, and enough stock to cover. Bring to a boil, and then decrease the heat to medium-low. Simmer, skimming often, for about 45 minutes, until the meat is fork-tender. Using a slotted spoon, transfer the meat to a bowl. Strain the stock though a fine-mesh sieve or colander and reserve. When cool enough to handle, shred the beef with a fork, discarding any pieces of fat or connective tissue.

Combine the pepper, oregano, basil, and paprika in a dry heavy saucepan over medium heat. Cook, stirring constantly, for 5 to 7 minutes, until toasted. Add the shredded beef and salsa and increase the heat to medium-high. Bring to a boil, stirring the meat with a fork to shred any remaining chunks. Cook for about 10 minutes, until the mixture comes to a rolling boil. Taste and adjust the seasoning with a pinch of salt if necessary. If the mixture appears dry, add some of the reserved stock to moisten. Serve immediately.

CHICKEN DESHEBRADA: Substitute 4 chicken hindquarters (leg and thigh) for the beef and decrease the cooking time to 35 minutes.

PORK DESHEBRADA: Substitute 1 pound boneless country-style pork ribs or shoulder for the beef. Cut the pork into 1-inch cubes. Add 1 roasted, peeled, seeded, and diced poblano chile with the flavorings.

Venison with Juniper and Wild Huckleberry

Sauce |||

Hunters from the Rocky Mountains to the Cascades and throughout the Great Lakes and eastern woodlands have long prepared game birds, venison, and other types of wild game over a fire of juniper. This modern interpretation combines the ageless harmony of juniper and venison with wild huckleberries and a few twenty-first century embellishments. Caribou, elk, moose, antelope, buffalo, duck, pigeon, and beef can be used interchangeably in this recipe with fabulous results. Choose fresh, in-season red meats from your area. If you have a hunter in the family, venison will surely be available to you in the fall. If not, many specialty meat shops can order it for you. ||| Serve this dish with root vegetables grilled alongside the meat or, better yet, grilled in a pan under the meat to capture the intense flavors from the meat drippings. A simple salad of wild cress, wild mustard, or miner's lettuce dressed with nut oil and fresh lemon juice would make this a complete and memorable meal. This preparation is best suited to those folks who like their meat rare to medium. If you prefer your meat well cooked, try another recipe; venison becomes very dry, tough, and stringy when cooked beyond medium. ||| SERVES 4 TO 6

2 pounds domestic deer leg meat, loin cuts, or rib chops

$1/4$ cup plus 2 tablespoons corn oil

2 tablespoons juniper berries, crushed

1 small tomato, chopped

1 (3-inch) piece licorice fern root, or $1/4$ teaspoon fennel seed, or 1 sprig fennel

$1/4$ cup coarsely chopped white onion

2 tablespoons coarsely chopped carrot

$1/2$ cup Zinfandel or Pinot Noir

2 cups venison brown stock (page 208)

1 teaspoon honey

1 tablespoon apple cider vinegar

$1/2$ cup fresh or frozen tart blue huckleberries

Have your butcher remove the meat from the bone and ask to have the bones cut into manageable pieces that will fit into your saucepan. Trim the meat to remove the sinew and connective tissue and reserve the bones for the brown stock.

Cut the meat into 4 to 6 pieces. Pour the $1/4$ cup oil into a shallow bowl and roll the meat in the oil to coat lightly. Evenly sprinkle the juniper over the meat. Cover the meat loosely with plastic wrap and refrigerate for at least 4 hours or overnight.

To prepare the sauce, combine the 2 tablespoons oil, the tomato, licorice root, onion, and carrot in a heavy saucepan over medium-high heat. Cook, stirring frequently, for about 10 minutes, until the vegetables take on a rich, deep dark brown color. Be careful not to allow them to burn. Add the wine and bring to a boil, then decrease the heat to medium. Cook for 10 to 12 minutes, until reduced by half. Increase the heat to high, add the stock, and return to a boil. Decrease the heat to medium-low and maintain a gentle simmer.

Place the honey, vinegar, and berries in a separate saucepan over high heat. Bring to a hard boil, and then decrease the heat to medium. Strain the

(CONTINUED)

Wood chips soaked in water, if using
a charcoal grill

Sea or kosher salt

Freshly ground black pepper

sauce into the honey and berry reduction and discard the solids. Simmer the sauce over medium heat for about 30 minutes, until reduced and thickened to the consistency of heavy cream.

Prepare a hot fire in a charcoal grill or preheat half of a gas grill to high. If using a charcoal grill, place the wood chips in a pile on the coals, but not directly in the center. This gives the chips enough exposure to the coals that they will smoke but not burn. Sprinkle the meat with salt and pepper and place on the grill rack over indirect heat. Cover the grill and cook for 7 to 12 minutes for medium-rare. Remove the meat from the grill and let relax for at least 10 minutes before cutting.

To serve, slice the meat across the grain and place on a warm platter. Serve the sauce on the side or spoon over the meat.

GRILLED CARIBOU CHOPS: Substitute 4 caribou loin or rib chops for the deer.

GRILLED MOOSE SIRLOIN: Substitute 2 pounds of trimmed moose sirloin cut into 4 steaks for the deer.

BRAISED LAMB SHANKS

||| This dish is based on Pueblo and Navajo ways of preparing lamb, mutton, or goat. Venison and buffalo are fine substitutes in this recipe. If using mutton, the cooking time will need to be extended by another hour or so. For a more traditional flavor, add 5 to 6 crushed juniper berries and about 1 tablespoon New Mexican chile powder or 1 Hatch or other mild green chile. Serve with crusty bread or Fry Bread (page 150). ||| SERVES 4

4 small tomatoes

4 cups brown stock or chicken brown stock (page 208)

2 tablespoons sunflower, corn, or safflower oil

4 lamb foreshanks

Sea or kosher salt

Freshly ground black pepper

12 cloves garlic

1 small white onion, sliced

2 tablespoons tomato paste

4 bay leaves

6 sprigs marjoram

1 cup fresh mint leaves, including tender stems

Prepare a hot fire in a charcoal grill, preheat a gas grill to high, or preheat the broiler. Place the tomatoes on the grill rack or in a broiler pan and cook, turning often, for 4 to 5 minutes, until the skins are slightly blackened and blistered. Peel the tomatoes and chop coarsely.

Place the stock in a saucepan and bring to a boil over high heat. Decrease the heat to low and keep hot.

Heat the oil in a braising pan over medium-high heat (for tips on braising, see page 203). Season the lamb liberally with salt and pepper. Add the meat to the pan and cook, turning, for 10 to 12 minutes, until browned on all sides. Add the garlic and onion and cook, stirring, for about 5 minutes, until the onion is slightly browned. Add the tomatoes, stock, tomato paste, bay leaves, marjoram, and mint. Increase the heat to high and bring to a full boil.

Cover the pan with a tight-fitting lid and decrease the heat to low. Gently simmer for about 2 hours, turning the meat 2 or 3 times to ensure even cooking. The meat should be fork-tender and easily come away from the bone.

This dish is best prepared early in the day and left to cool completely so that the meat relaxes. Before serving, reheat in a 350°F oven for 20 to 30 minutes. This makes for the tenderest lamb. Preparing the dish a day ahead and reheating it the next day would also work well. At the very least, plan to let the shanks rest, covered and in a warm place, for about 20 minutes before serving.

BRAISED BUFFALO SHANKS: Substitute about 2 pounds buffalo shank for the lamb.

BRAISED VENISON SHANKS: Substitute 3-inch-thick venison shank pieces, 2 to 3 per person, for the lamb. Omit the mint and add 6 juniper berries and 4 sage leaves.

GREAT BASIN–STYLE BRAISED RABBIT ||| Rabbit continues to be a

favored food among many indigenous people throughout the Americas. It was a staple for the Utes and Shoshone of the Great Basin. New potatoes, such as those used in this dish, are also a Great Basin delicacy. ||| This recipe borrows flavors from the Mescalero Apache, Pueblo, and Shoshone peoples. It was inspired by the Shoshone method of preparing boiled rabbit, accompanied by bitterroot, camas, wild onions, or wild carrots. Zelda Tillman and her mother, Margie Tillman, of Wyoming, were very helpful in sharing their perspectives on Shoshone foods both past and present. Zelda's fry bread recipe helped in the development of the one in this book (page 150). Serve this rabbit with chochoyotes (page 19) or Grill Bread (page 150). ||| SERVES 4

4 cups white stock (page 209) or canned
    chicken stock

2 cups water

1/4 cup sunflower, corn, or safflower oil

4 pairs rabbit hindquarters (legs and
    thighs)

1 leek, coarsely chopped

2 carrots, peeled and cut into 1/4-inch slices

1 white onion, sliced

3 to 4 cloves garlic, finely chopped

2 mild green Hatch or Anaheim chiles,
    seeded and coarsely chopped

4 bay leaves

1 sprig marjoram, or 1/4 teaspoon
    dried marjoram

1 sprig oregano, or 1/4 teaspoon dried
    oregano

1/4 bunch cilantro

1/2 teaspoon ground cumin

1 tablespoon black peppercorns, crushed

1/2 teaspoon sea or kosher salt

1 1/4 pounds new potatoes, quartered

Place the stock and water in a saucepan and bring to a boil over high heat. Decrease the heat to low and keep warm.

Heat the oil in a braising pan over high heat (for tips on braising, see page 203). Add the rabbit and cook, turning once, for about 7 minutes on each side, until browned. Add the leek, carrots, onion, garlic, and chiles and cook, stirring often, for about 5 minutes, until the vegetables are softened but not browned. Add the stock, bay leaves, marjoram, oregano, cilantro, cumin, peppercorns, and salt. Bring to a rapid boil.

Cover the pan with a tight-fitting lid and decrease the heat to low. Gently simmer for about 1 hour, turning the meat 2 or 3 times to ensure even cooking. Add the potatoes and cook for about 30 minutes, until the meat is fork-tender and easily comes away from the bone and the potatoes are tender. Remove and discard the bay leaves, marjoram, oregano, and cilantro. Serve immediately.

NAVAJO BRAISED RABBIT WITH BEANS AND HOMINY: After browning the rabbit, add 2 teaspoons of New Mexican chile powder, 1 1/2 cups of cooked hominy, and 2 cups of cooked pinto beans. Increase the water from 2 cups to 4 cups.

COLOMBIAN-STYLE RABBIT WITH COCONUT MILK |||

Coconuts are abundant throughout the northern regions of South America and they figure into the cookery of many dishes. When simmered slowly with coconut, annatto, peppers, and spicy chiles, rabbit can become a deeply gratifying regional specialty. ||| SERVES 4

2 small tomatoes

3 cups white stock (page 209)

2 cups unsweetened coconut milk

3 tablespoons annatto oil (page 210)

4 pairs rabbit hindquarters (legs and thighs)

1 red bell pepper, sliced

1 green bell pepper, sliced

1 white onion, sliced

3 to 4 cloves garlic, finely chopped

2 serrano chiles

1/2 teaspoon sea or kosher salt

1/2 teaspoon freshly ground black pepper

1 tablespoon tomato paste

Prepare a hot fire in a charcoal grill, preheat a gas grill to high, or preheat the broiler. Place the tomatoes on the grill rack or in a broiler pan and cook, turning often, for 4 to 5 minutes, until the skins are slightly blackened and blistered. Peel the tomatoes and chop coarsely.

Place the stock and coconut milk in a saucepan and bring to a boil over high heat. Decrease the heat to low and keep warm.

Heat the oil in a braising pan over high heat (for tips on braising, see page 203). Add the rabbit and cook, turning once, for about 7 minutes on each side, until browned. Add the red and green peppers, onion, garlic, and chiles and cook, stirring often, for about 5 minutes, until the vegetables are softened but not browned. Add the stock-coconut mixture, salt, and black pepper. Bring to a rapid boil, and then decrease the heat to low. As it simmers, add the tomatoes and tomato paste, stirring to fully dissolve the tomato paste.

Cover the pan with a tight-fitting lid and maintain a very low simmer. Gently simmer for about 1 1/2 hours, turning the meat 2 or 3 times to ensure even cooking. The dish is ready when the meat is fork-tender and easily comes away from the bone. Remove and discard the chiles. Serve immediately.

PORK IN OAXACAN MOLE VERDE

||| While chicken is commonly prepared with this sauce, pork may also be used and is particularly well suited to this recipe. Mole verde is one of seven mole sauces typical of Oaxaca, Mexico. However, as for most of the classic dishes in this book, there are variations. Some cooks exclude the sesame seeds, some prefer different spices, and still others omit the lettuce and chard. This mole has a complex flavor and a lovely green hue. Adding chochoyotes (page 19) right at the end of the cooking is a terrific, though untraditional, embellishment. ||| SERVES 6

3 pounds pork shoulder or boneless country-style ribs, trimmed and cut into 1-inch cubes

1 bay leaf

1- to 2-inch piece canela or cinnamon

5 whole peppercorns

1 small white onion, coarsely chopped

4 cups white stock (page 209)

1½ tablespoons dried Mexican oregano or marjoram

4 whole cloves

¼ teaspoon cumin seed

¼ teaspoon anise seed

4 allspice berries

½ cup pumpkin seeds

½ cup sesame seeds

6 to 8 tomatillos (about ½ pound), husked and coarsely chopped

2 jalapeño chiles, coarsely chopped

6 cloves garlic

½ white onion, quartered

3 cups water

¼ cup corn oil

¼ cup fresh masa, or 2 tablespoons masa harina

½ teaspoon sea or kosher salt

Place the pork, bay leaf, canela, peppercorns, chopped onion, and stock in a large saucepan. Bring to a rapid boil over high heat, then decrease the heat to medium-low. Simmer for about 40 minutes, stirring from time to time and skimming the surface of the broth with a slotted spoon to remove impurities as they accumulate. The pork should yield easily when pierced with a fork. Transfer the pork to a plate and keep warm. Pass the broth through a fine-mesh sieve and reserve.

Combine the oregano, cloves, cumin, anise, and allspice in a dry sauté pan over medium-high heat. Cook, stirring constantly, for 3 to 4 minutes, until lightly toasted. Transfer to a bowl. Add the pumpkin seeds to the sauté pan and cook, stirring constantly, for 5 minutes, or until they swell but do not brown. Add the pumpkin seeds to the spices in the bowl. Add the sesame seeds to the sauté pan and swirl and toss for 3 to 5 minutes, until golden brown. Add the sesame seeds to the spices and pumpkin seeds and toss to combine. Transfer the seeds and spices to a blender and add about 1 cup of the reserved pork broth. Process until smooth, scraping the sides and adding additional broth if necessary.

Place the tomatillos, chiles, garlic, quartered onion, and 1½ cups of the water in a food processor or blender. Process until smooth. Heat the oil in a saucepan over medium-high heat. Add the puréed tomatillo mixture and cook, stirring often, for 6 to 7 minutes, until slightly reduced. Add the spice and seed mixture and simmer, stirring, for about 15 minutes. In a bowl, blend the masa with 1 cup of the reserved pork broth. Add the masa mixture, 1 cup of the pork broth, and the salt to the tomatillo sauce. Cook, stirring frequently, for about 10 minutes.

(CONTINUED)

2 tablespoons coarsely chopped epazote

4 green leaf or romaine lettuce leaves

4 leaves Swiss chard

1/2 cup coarsely chopped cilantro

1/4 cup coarsely chopped flat-leaf parsley

Combine the epazote, lettuce, chard, cilantro, parsley, and the remaining 1 1/2 cups water in a food processor or blender and blend until smooth.

Add the pork and vegetable purée to the sauce. Simmer for about 7 minutes, until warmed through, thinning the sauce with additional pork broth if too thick. Serve immediately.

CHICKEN IN GREEN MOLE: Substitute 1 (3 1/2- to 4-pound) stewing hen for the pork. Cut the chicken into 8 pieces.

TURKEY IN GREEN MOLE: Substitute 1 turkey hindquarter (leg and thigh) for the pork.

WILD BOAR LOIN ROAST ||| Wild boar are not as large as farmed pigs, so the loin is much smaller than pork loin and requires less cooking time. After marinating the meat, little more than simple roasting is required. Wild boar is a delightful alternative meat, well worth offering to family and friends throughout the year. ||| Wild boar procured from a reliable source, such as the Texas Wild Game Cooperative's Broken Arrow Ranch, will ensure that the boar is safe from food-borne illness. See sources, page 214. ||| SERVES 4 TO 6

1/4 cup sugar

2 tablespoons sea or kosher salt

2 tablespoons minced wild onion or shallots

2 cloves garlic, minced

1 tablespoon finely minced thyme

1 tablespoon finely minced sweet cicely tops or fennel tops

2 1/2 pounds wild boar loin meat, trimmed

Combine the sugar, salt, onion, garlic, thyme, and sweet cicely in a bowl and mix with a wooden spoon. Place the boar on a rack in a roasting pan and distribute the seasoning mixture over the meat. Loosely cover with plastic wrap and refrigerate for 4 hours or overnight.

Preheat the oven to 450°F. Remove the rack and meat from the roasting pan and pour off the excess liquid in the bottom of the pan. Rinse the pan and wipe it dry. Return the rack and meat to the pan. Place in the oven and roast for about 10 minutes. Decrease the heat to 350°F and cook for about 10 minutes for rare, or until the desired doneness. Transfer to a cutting board, slice, and serve at once.

PORK LOIN ROAST: Replace the wild boar with 2 1/2 pounds trimmed pork loin and increase the roasting time at 350°F to about 45 minutes.

YUCATÁN-STYLE PORK ||| This recipe is an adaptation of a traditional Maya dish that

would have featured wild boar or venison. The red achiote paste, or *recado,* is made from crushed annatto seeds, garlic, herbs, and other seasonings. This recipe calls for a commercially made achiote paste sold as *condimento achiote,* which is widely available at Latin markets and in grocery stores. Traditionally, the flavored and wrapped meats are buried under a smoldering fire in a pit to cook. Be sure to sample this dish if you are in the Yucatán Peninsula of Mexico, where it is a classic. This version is a close approximation, though it lacks the earthy elements associated with pit cookery. Preparing this dish over a slow barbecue with a tight-fitting lid creates excellent results, although the cooking time is less predictable. Serve with Pickled Red Onions (page 40), tortillas, and black beans. ||| SERVES 4

2 pounds pork shoulder or boneless
    country-style pork ribs

$1/4$ cup achiote paste

2 cloves garlic, minced

Juice of 1 lime

Juice of 1 orange

Juice of 1 grapefruit

1 teaspoon sea or kosher salt

2 banana leaves, for cooking

$1/4$ cup olive oil, melted pork fat, or lard

If using pork shoulder, trim the pork of excess fat and connective tissue and cut into generous pieces. In a bowl, combine the achiote paste with the garlic and citrus juices and mix well. Add the pork and sprinkle with the salt. Toss until the pork is completely coated. Cover and place in the refrigerator for at least 4 hours or overnight.

Preheat the oven to 375°F. Line a baking sheet with the banana leaves, providing generous overhang. Place the pork pieces on the leaves and pour any remaining seasoning paste over the top. Drizzle the oil over the meat and fold the banana leaves over the pork to completely cover. Tuck the leaves under the pork to secure. Cover the baking sheet with aluminum foil.

Place the pan in the oven and bake for about 2 hours, until the pork is fork-tender. Remove the pan from the oven. Using a spatula, transfer the package to a serving platter. With a fork, pull the meat apart into serving pieces. Pour the cooking liquid into a gravy dish and pass separately with the meat.

YUCATÁN-STYLE CHICKEN: Replace the pork with 1 ($3^1/_2$- to 4-pound) stewing hen cut into 8 pieces.

BRAZILIAN COZIDO ||| This beautiful stew, a mere five to six hundred years new to the indigenous peoples of Brazil, is nonetheless a staple there now. Variations of this simple-to-prepare dish are found in kitchens throughout the region. New World ingredients unique to the Americas distinguish this dish from the Portuguese original. *Farofa,* or toasted manioc flour resembling bread crumbs, is blended with some of the cooking liquid (called *pirão* at this point) and then reincorporated into the broth. The pirão thickens the liquids and helps concentrate the flavor. ||| SERVES 4

2 tablespoons corn oil

2 beef short ribs with bones

4 bacon slices, cut into ½-inch pieces

1 bay leaf

Pinch of freshly ground black pepper

4 cups brown stock (page 208) or canned
    beef stock

½ pound linguiça sausage,
    cut into 4 pieces

VEGETABLES
2 tablespoons corn oil

1 small white onion, cut into 8 wedges

1 large carrot, peeled and cut into
    ½-inch slices

1 large sweet potato, peeled and
    cut into 8 wedges

½ pound okra (about 8 pieces), trimmed

1 chayote squash, seed included,
    cut into 8 wedges

½ pound string beans, stringed

½ small head cabbage, cut into 2-inch
    chunks

1 plantain, peeled and cut into 8 pieces

1 ear corn, shucked and cut into 4 pieces

¼ teaspoon sea or kosher salt

Pinch of freshly ground black pepper

Heat the oil in a large soup pot over high heat. Add the ribs and cook, turning, for 10 to 12 minutes, until browned on both sides. Add the bacon, bay leaf, pepper, and stock. Bring to a boil, then decrease the heat to medium-low. Cook at a low simmer for about 1½ hours, skimming off the impurities as they accumulate with a slotted spoon and turning the meat from time to time. Add the sausage and cook for about 30 minutes, until the beef yields easily when pierced with a fork. Transfer the meat to a plate, cover, and keep warm. Strain the broth into a bowl, skim off the excess fat, and reserve.

To cook the vegetables, heat the oil in the pot used to cook the meats over medium-high heat. Add the onion, carrot, and sweet potato and cook, stirring often, for about 7 minutes, until softened but not browned. Add the reserved broth, the okra, squash, beans, cabbage, plantain, corn, salt, and pepper to the pan. Bring to a boil and then decrease the heat to medium-low. Cook at a low simmer for about 20 minutes. Add the meat and decrease the heat to low so that the meat steeps in the liquid.

PIQUANT SAUCE

1/2 cup fruity olive oil

Juice of 4 limes

1 malagueta chile or any small hot chile, seeded and finely chopped

1/2 red onion, minced

4 cloves garlic, pressed or minced

1/4 cup minced flat-leaf parsley

Pinch of sea or kosher salt

Pinch of freshly ground black pepper

1/4 cup manioc flour or fine breadcrumbs

To prepare the sauce, whisk together the olive oil and lime juice in a bowl. Add the chile, red onion, garlic, parsley, salt, and pepper and mix well. Allow the sauce to stand at room temperature.

To serve, arrange the meat and vegetables in a casserole. Pour the broth into a separate warm crock or bowl with a ladle. Heat 4 soup plates and spoon 1 tablespoon of the manioc flour into each. At the table, guests should ladle some hot broth into their bowls and stir in the manioc to form a pirão. The meat and vegetables should then be spooned over the pirão and eaten with the sauce on the side.

CALDO |||

To the Mexican cook, *caldo* is a soulful preparation that begins with roasting the chiles, tomatoes, and onions and ends with a simply prepared meal that is extremely satisfying. If you do not have an indoor grill or are unable to roast the peppers, tomatoes, and onion over an open fire, don't worry; this dish is very good without this traditional step. ||| Most any type of cooked dry beans, such as black, pinto, or garbanzo, are also good additions to this dish. Feel free to substitute your favorite vegetable or those in season. The stew is especially good served with cooked white rice, salsa, hot sauce, and plenty of warm tortillas. ||| SERVES 4 TO 6

1 poblano chile

2 tomatoes, halved

1 white onion, quartered

1/4 cup corn oil

4 chicken thighs

4 country-style pork ribs (optional)

Sea or kosher salt

Freshly ground black pepper

4 fresh chorizo sausages

1 ham hock

1/4 cup tomato purée

2 cloves garlic, minced

2 carrots, peeled and cut into 8 pieces

1/2 pound wild or cultivated mushrooms,
   quartered

2 ears sweet corn, each cut into 3 pieces

2 limes, halved

1/4 cup coarsely chopped cilantro,
   for garnish

Place the chile, tomatoes, and onion on a hot grill or directly over a flame and cook, turning as needed, for 3 to 4 minutes, until the skins of the chile and tomatoes blacken slightly and blister and the onion softens in its own smoke. Place the chile in a plastic bag to steam. Peel, seed, and chop the tomatoes. Peel, stem, and seed the chile. Cut the chile into strips.

Heat the oil in a large heavy soup pot over medium heat. Season the chicken and pork with salt and pepper. Add the chicken and pork to the pot and cook, turning once, for about 10 minutes, until browned. Add the chorizo, ham hock, tomato purée, garlic, carrots, mushrooms, and corn and enough water to cover. Bring to a boil and then decrease the heat to low and simmer gently. Skim the surface with a slotted spoon to remove any impurities that accumulate. Cover and cook for about 40 minutes, until the meat is tender when pierced with a fork. Add the grilled vegetables and simmer for about 12 minutes, until warmed through.

To serve, transfer the caldo to a casserole or serving bowl. Squeeze the limes over the stew and sprinkle with the cilantro. Serve immediately.

BEEF CALDO WITH TRIPE: Omit the chicken and pork and substitute 4 beef short ribs and 1 pound of prepared tripe, cut into 1/2-inch pieces.

São Paulo Churrasco

||| A traditional barbecue (*churrasco*) consists of large pieces of beef cooked on stakes at a pit fire and served on skewers. This interpretation makes the preparation more manageable in your kitchen. If you do have a fire pit or traditional barbecue, by all means use it. ||| SERVES 4

Zest of 1 lemon

1/4 cup olive oil

Sea or kosher salt

Freshly ground black pepper

2 cloves garlic, pressed or minced

1/2 teaspoon crushed red peppers

4 (6- to 8-ounce) rib or New York sirloin
    steaks

DIPPING SAUCE
Juice of 1 lemon

1/4 teaspoon crushed red peppers

1 large white onion, minced

2 tablespoons chopped flat-leaf parsley

Place the zest in a small saucepan with water to cover. Place over high heat and bring to a boil. Drain and repeat the process 2 more times. Rinse the zest with cold water, pat dry, and chop.

Place the olive oil in a shallow baking dish. Stir in the zest, salt, pepper, garlic, and red peppers. Roll the steaks in the marinade, cover, and refrigerate overnight.

Prepare a hot fire in a charcoal grill or preheat a gas grill to high.

To prepare the sauce, combine all of the ingredients in a bowl and mix well.

Place the meat on the grill rack and cook, turning once, for 7 to 10 minutes on each side, until cooked to your liking. Remove from the heat and allow the meat to rest for 10 minutes before serving. Serve with the dipping sauce on the side.

Reservation Foods

INSTEAD OF FOCUSING ON PLAINS INDIAN foods of the buffalo days or the quick foods of today, my best memories concentrate on what we ate when I was a child on the Fort Belknap Indian Reservation in Montana, at least sixty years ago. Several overlapping conditions contributed to our menu, and—in an opposite way—continue to do so today. First, those Indian families that lived away from any federal government agency and had no electricity, automobiles, or even running water, were—by today's standards—poverty stricken. But we didn't see ourselves that way because we lived from the land, we knew no one who had a real, long-lasting job, and periodically we received government rations. Although my grandmother Clementine, whose Indian name was Singing Rock, raised several of us siblings, she also raised some chickens. We had fresh eggs, but I remember clearly the first time the rations included powdered eggs. She mixed the powder with water, fried the mass in a hot skillet, and it changed into scrambled eggs. They were delicious.

Indian tradition determined our diet as well, and it followed a strict seasonal cycle, because we had no electricity or even iceboxes to help preserve our food. We could not get complete sustenance from nature, because the buffalo were gone, but additional consumables often took the hunger away. My grandmother had her sons and grandsons dig a root cellar under the one-room log cabin where we all lived. After the harvest in the fall, the potatoes stored there kept us going throughout the winter, augmented by the occasional deer meat that came our way and other foods that we had prepared and preserved. Fried potatoes are my favorite—some members of our large family preferred their portions with syrup on top. Our most reliable store-bought fruit dish consisted of canned tomatoes with sugar sprinkled on top. I can't help it, I still favor them today—they bring back fond memories.

Another essential element came in the shape of a wheel—wheel bread or, as the miners called it, bannock bread. Most peoples have such a bread. Ours took form after mixing flour, baking powder, a bit of salt, some lard, and water together. The thick dough was kneaded into a big, fat tortilla shape and placed into a medium-hot, dry skillet to cook. After a short time it was turned over and cooked until it was finished. Pieces could be broken off according to one's hunger and eaten hot or smeared with what one could call poor man's butter—a layer of lard with salt lightly sprinkled over it. Our Uncle Charlie always preferred wheel bread to most others, because he said store-bought bread tasted flat and felt like foam.

June berries and fry bread are gifts from the One Above. Every group of people has a favorite food that is identified with them. For the French it may be escargots; for Russians, borscht; and for Mexicans, tortillas. For us the magic food is fry bread.

There is little special about the mixture for the dough. It can be used for loafs, biscuits, or anything. In my younger days, cooks used baking powder (Calumet brand, with the Indian-head logo) as the leavening agent to make the product lighter. Today, as cooks become gourmets, many use a yeast mixture that produces the desired puffiness and adds a special aroma that blends easily with the taste.

There are many secrets to making the perfect fry bread, which varies from group to group. After the dough is made it is rolled into a sheet about 1/2 inch thick. Many tribes in the north cut the sheet into rectangles of about 4 by 5 inches. A slit is cut in the center of each piece to help cook the interior evenly. Finally, in the north, each piece is slightly pulled and stretched in transverse directions and placed into the hot grease.

Another secret of making special fry bread lies in the grease. Long ago everyone used lard, but today they use liquid cooking oil, or better yet, a solid shortening such as Crisco. The solid shortening can be heated to a higher temperature, allowing the fry bread to cook faster so it won't absorb as much of the grease. My wife experimented with using the healthier olive oil, but the toughness of the outer surface discouraged us. Besides, it just didn't taste right.

The grease must be hot and deep enough so that when the dough is placed in the pan it pops up to the surface and is free to float as it expands. If the dough just stays at the bottom of the pan, the grease is not hot enough. A test piece dropped into the hot grease will be active and scoot around to let you know the temperature is right.

After the piece has cooked awhile, the underside will begin to brown. When it reaches a golden hue, put a fork under it and carefully turn it over and let it cook until both sides are the same color. After it cools slightly, taste it, and adjust things if necessary. When it is perfect your taste buds will know. By spreading meat sauce over the top of the fry bread, adding some fresh, chopped lettuce and tomatoes, and spooning on some spicy salsa, you have created a masterpiece called an Indian taco.

Few Indian people dispute that the Navajo people in the Southwest produce the best fry bread by far: they cut big pieces of dough and slap it around between their palms to knead and flatten it before placing it into the grease. The results are large, light, bulbous, and delicious.

The most stable staple of our dietary survival is bean soup. The beans can be either Great Northern or navy beans, and the first step in the cooking process is inspecting them, sorting out small stones that would break a tooth. Next, my grandmother would soak the beans in water overnight, perhaps to soften them or allow them to give off gas, and then she would cook them throughout the next day. In the meantime she would retrieve a slab of bacon rind she had saved and cut it into wide strips, which she added to the soup at the proper time. After breathing in its delicious aroma for several hours, we were more than ready when it was finally done. With a little salt added and some bread alongside, the meal was complete. My wife and I still have the same combination whenever we can; my wife uses large chunks of smoked ham hocks instead of the bacon rind.

Indian people love to eat meat. This trait may come from the fact that we ate parts of the buffalo, in its many forms, for centuries. When buffalo were nearly exterminated in the latter part of the 1800s, we turned to the other available meat—government beef rations provided by the treaties in which we gave up portions of our lands. Today buffalo meat is relatively rare (no pun intended), and is considered a delicacy.

The very best type of meat, as everyone knows, is fried steak, but that is not unique to our people, so it will not be described here. Because of the lack of refrigeration, we developed dry meat. It is a simple solution to the problem of preserving meat. After the meat is sliced into thin pieces with the grain of the flesh it is washed in salt water and allowed to dry on high racks that keep the dogs from getting it. Sometimes the slices are hung in smoke to keep the flies away. When the meat is dried into a hard, stiff form on both sides, it is put away until much later. Dry meat can be eaten in two basic ways. The most common way is to boil the pieces in water, with a few potatoes or Indian turnips. The meat never really softens, but it is nourishing and tasty.

Another traditional way to eat dry meat is to make it into pemmican. When the time arrived for the processing, my grandmother would find a square piece of canvas, drape it over a small wooden "pounding board," and place this equipment under a nice shade tree. Sitting comfortably, she would cradle the handle of a single-bitted axe under her arm near one end and, holding the other end near the head, would pound the dry meat pieces with the blunt side of the axe head until they were pulverized. She would place the fluffy chopped material into a container—usually a pillowcase—for storage, and continue the process for hours. Additional foods, such as berries or seeds, could be added to the pemmican, but we ate it straight. Consuming this very special food is interesting. The aroma is more notable than fragrant, and a pinch was the easiest way to obtain a quick and nourishing snack. Shaping lard into a small ball and rolling it in the pemmican could produce a larger portion. Gooood.

≋ Sioux (?) woman cooking. (N41458)

In the Northern Plains, whenever we have an outdoor ceremony or other cultural activity, we favor boiled meat. It is easy to cook, tasty, and can last a day or two without refrigeration. For an outdoor feast, the host has people build a fire around or under a large cast-iron kettle that is partially filled with water. After the meat is cut into pieces about 3 inches square, it is placed in the boiling vat for about 15 to 20 minutes and then removed. The layers of meat and fat can be seen and the meat is firm rather than falling apart. Although it requires some salting, it is tasty and travels easily when the guests take some home. And, of course, other things are added to the broth, rendering it into delicious soup.

The two primary foods that are the mainstay of our traditional seasonal diets are the fruits of the Plains: chokecherries (*Prunus virginiana* L.) and June berries (*Amelanchier alnifolia* Nutt.). In the spring one can see the appropriate bushes budding. On occasion while out playing we might attempt to eat a green chokecherry, but we would mostly regret it. Chokecherries not only stain the front teeth, as there is little fruit on the immature cherry, but the juice actually causes a tightening of the throat that makes swallowing difficult. We would break the pit and savor its tasty white center. Although it is said that the pit and leaves contain cyanide, a poison, it never harmed us. Non-Indians can and even sell chokecherry jam, but it does not contain the essence of the fruit that lies in the center of the pit.

When they ripen in late August or early September, chokecherries are purple. After picking and eating many as they came off the bush, we allowed most of them to make their way to my grandmother. After thoroughly washing them, she would cook the cherries before grinding them in a meat grinder to break the pits. It is said that cooking neutralizes the cyanide. When the seeds were broken and the cherries mashed she would make patties or a thick soup out of the aggregate. The dried patties could last forever and be used for soup, but one had to remember not to crunch down too hard on the mixture.

Gooseberries (*Ribes* species, Saxifrage family) look like translucent, fingernail-sized watermelons, green with stripes. We tasted them too, but they are bitter until the fall. They are difficult to pick because they grow on bushes covered with sharp stickers, and they are really not worth it, although some people like to can them.

Another snack came from the so-called buffalo berry (*Shepherdia argentea* Nutt.). They are small, either red or orange, and grow on a gray bush. They are difficult to pick because large thorns protect them. They ripen in mid-August but are not harvested until after the first frost. At that time canvas is spread underneath and the bush is struck until the berries fall into the canvas. People can these berries as well. Because no cattle existed on the Northern Plains before non-Indians arrived, whenever the Indian people said "bull," they meant buffalo bull, so we call the buffalo berries "bull berries."

By far the best prairie fruit of them all are June berries. In the same family as the blueberry, these sweet, succulent treats are also known as serviceberries, sarvice berries, Saskatoon berries, and by other terms. Although they flower in May and ripen in July, we call them June berries. The bushes seem to grow some distance from the road, but the berries are easy to pick because they are not too high and the fruits are easily detached. The major drawback to picking June berries is that they are relatively rare and so delicious that not too many of them make it home—the pickers gorge themselves on them. Those that do make it home can be eaten raw on the spot, sun-dried for later use, or thickened with cornstarch and made into a sweet soup.

It is not easy being an Indian and having to deal with diabetes, racism, and all the rest, but The One

Above, in his infinite wisdom, seemingly struck a balance with us. In exchange for all the difficulties we endure, He gave us fry bread and June berries.

Sixty years ago, beverages didn't have the importance they have today. Tepid water from the large barrel outside was the only beverage available to the kids, and the adults favored black pekoe tea. Neither coffee nor soda pop had yet made the scene.

There are other traditional foods, but they are limited to special events, such as ceremonies and Sun Dances, where there are elders. Some of these foods include tripe, especially the "many folds" part, boiled pup, and raw kidney.

Most reservation Indian people view a wake, which takes place the night before a funeral, as an important community event, almost a social occasion. The people slowly gather in the evening, usually bringing foods that span the full range of salads, chicken, fruits, chips, bread, and cakes. The family of the deceased is responsible for providing other vitals, such as June berry or chokecherry soup, dry meat soup, boiling meat, other traditional foods, and cigarettes. Soon a priest conducts a brief service and the community pays its respects to the departed. Then the young people deliver fully laden plates, first to the elders and then to the others. While eating and afterward, the people visit, laugh, and enjoy themselves, sometimes all night. They are expected to have brought a pillowcase or other container in which to take food with them when they go home.

Today, as the elders pass on and Indian people are assimilating into the maelstrom of contemporary life, refrigerators are everywhere and the people can therefore preserve and eat anything. The traditional foods still appear, but they are rare because they cannot be purchased in a store. Few people have the time or energy to locate and harvest them from nature, so they are only cooked for meaningful events, such as cultural ceremonies, wakes, and funerals. These gatherings continue to bind the community together and allow us to maintain the traditional food customs that make us Indian people.

—George P. Horse Capture

George P. Horse Capture (A'aninin) was born on the Fort Belknap Indian Reservation in north-central Montana in 1937. He earned a B.A. in Anthropology from the University of California at Berkeley and an M.A. in History from Montana State University, Bozeman. In 1996, he was awarded an honorary Doctorate of Letters from the University of Montana. He is the author of *Powwow* and coauthor of *Beauty, Honor, and Tradition: The Legacy of Plains Indian Shirts.* He is the senior counselor to the director at the Smithsonian National Museum of the American Indian.

CHAPTER FIVE

GAME BIRDS
& FOWL

≋ Catawba man and boy hunting with a blowgun, 1922.
South Carolina. (N12398)

In the Arctic region, a young Inupiaq boy coming of age as a hunter has traditionally been expected to master the art of imitating the calls of ducks, geese, gulls, and auks, as well as the less common guillemots, kittiwakes, puffins, and razorbills. If the young hunter cannot call the birds with his voice, he makes whistles of wood, clay, antler, or bone to summon prey by imitating a courtship or distress call. Carved whistles and weapons are often adorned with an animal motif to please the hunted animal's spirit so it will return to earth and repopulate.

Before the introduction of firearms, Yup'ik hunters along the Bering Strait devised snares of rawhide and spruce roots to entangle unwary ducks and geese as they attempted to land or retreat through openings of shoreline and sea grasses. Similar devices were fashioned of whalebone along the inlets of Kotzebue and Norton Sounds, Kowak River, and Big Lake. In the Yukon Delta, the Yup'ik strung salmon nets with stout braces and hoisted them above shallow water. A human chain was formed some distance away from the net to drive the waterfowl into it.

In the North American interior, many tribes employed similar snares, nets, and slings to harvest ducks and geese that were molting at the end of the breeding season. Slings, or *bolas*, are made of various string-like materials. Stones or other heavy objects are tethered near the ends of the strings. One hurls the bola into the anticipated flight path of the bird and the strings are slung around and around, wrapping the prey and bringing it down. The Ojibwe around Bois Blanc Island in the Great Lakes region employed their own types of snares and slings during the seasons of migrating waterfowl, and the people of the Great Basin were ingenious in fashioning lifelike bird decoys out of wood or buoyant tule rushes, often covering them with feathered bird skins.

The blowgun was an important tool for hunting game birds and waterfowl throughout the Americas. Tribes of the southeastern United States fashioned blowguns from cane more than three feet in length. These blowguns were similar to those used today by Amazonian tribes. Blowguns may have been introduced to the Northern Hemisphere from Central America via the Yucatán or across the Caribbean archipelago. Today, darts are held in a type of quiver called a *tunta* by the Shuar/Achuar people in Ecuador. Pieces of natural cotton fiber from the ceiba tree are wrapped around the darts to facilitate a smooth, direct flight path. The dart tips are dipped in a substance that stuns or kills the prey, and they are grooved to break easily on contact.

The Muscovy duck, *Cairina moschata,* was domesticated long before the Spanish arrived in South America. It is unknown whether domestication occurred during the pre-Inka period in Peru or in the eastern part of the continent, but when Columbus visited the West Indies, he reported seeing Native people tending goose-sized ducks.

Flavor, size, and fat content are the principal culinary differences between the many types of game birds and fowl, both domestic and wild. Field dressing—removing the skin and the feathers—is common among hunters of small wild birds. When presented with field-dressed birds, simply cover the breast with bacon or pork fat and tent the bird with foil prior to roasting.

Breasts of larger birds, such as duck, goose, and wild turkey, should be cooked apart from the leg and thigh since the dark meat takes longer to cook. The breast of some birds like duck and squab are best when eaten rare to medium, making the separation of the hindquarters from the breast a good option.

ROAST WILD GOOSE |||

Wild goose can be sumptuous and moist when lemons are inserted into the cavity before roasting, as they have a tenderizing effect. Many people combine a roasting and *poëlling* (roasting with the addition of liquid) method to ensure a tender goose. Often a bottle of wine or a quart of chicken broth is poured into the bottom of the pan after the first high-heat session. The resulting liquid is used to baste the bird, then strained, skimmed of fat, and turned into a delicious sauce, either by reduction or by adding some cornstarch. Serve with wild rice, succotash, or your favorite stuffing. ||| SERVES 4

1 ($2^{1}/_{2}$- to 3-pound) wild goose, cleaned

2 tablespoons sea or kosher salt

About $^{1}/_{2}$ teaspoon freshly ground black pepper

1 lemon, quartered (optional)

4 wild onions, trimmed and sliced (about 1 cup), or 1 cup sliced white onion

2 crab apples, quartered, or 1 tart green apple, quartered

1 wild or domestic celery stalk, sliced

1 bay leaf

Place the goose in a soup pot and add water to completely cover. Remove the goose from the pot and measure the salt into the water. Whisk to completely dissolve the salt. Return the goose to the pot, cover, and refrigerate overnight.

Preheat the oven to 425°F.

Remove the goose from the brine, rinse with cold water, and pat dry. Discard the brine.

Open the goose vent and season the cavity with the pepper. Place the lemon, onions, apples, celery, and bay leaf in the cavity. Tuck the wing tips behind the backbone and tie the legs closed with kitchen twine. Place the goose on a rack in a roasting pan. Place in the oven and roast for about 45 minutes, until the fat renders.

Decrease the oven temperature to 350°F. Remove the goose from the oven and place the roasting pan on a heat-resistant surface. Prick the skin (not the flesh) of the breast with the tip of a thin knife or the tines of a meat fork from top to bottom and side to side to allow excess fat to drain. Hold the pricking utensil at an angle pointing away from you, lifting the skin while piercing it slightly rather than employing a stabbing motion.

Return the goose to the oven and roast for $2^{1}/_{2}$ to 3 hours, basting often with the rendered drippings. To determine if the goose is cooked, insert the tines of a meat fork into the thigh. If the liquid runs clear, remove the bird from the oven and let it rest for at least 20 minutes prior to carving.

Slice the meat into serving portions and arrange on a platter. Serve immediately.

ROAST DOMESTIC GOOSE: Use a 6- to 8-pound goose to serve 6 to 8. Prior to brining, remove the excess fat from inside the neck and breast cavity. Decrease the final roasting time to $1^{1}/_{2}$ to 2 hours.

WILD GOOSE WITH SAUERKRAUT AND JUNIPER ||| Tribes

throughout the Arctic region from Alaska to Newfoundland harvest wood sorrel (*Oxalis* sp.), although it has a very short season there and is difficult to find. Some elders warn against eating too much of it because wood sorrel contains oxalic acid, and its tartness may cause an upset stomach. However, it is delicious when fermented in vinegar to make a kind of sauerkraut and used to accompany braised or roasted meats. Here, sauerkraut made of cabbage is used to make the dish more accessible to home cooks. ||| The Alsatians of France make a similar dish that is a regional classic there, although they add wine and sausages. Lacking a wild goose, this recipe is quite good with sausages alone. Serve with a simple salad of new greens dressed with Wild Flower Honey Vinaigrette (page 46). Warm Cattail Cakes (page 165) are a nice accompaniment. ||| SERVES 4

1 (2½- to 3-pound) wild goose, cleaned

¼ teaspoon sea or kosher salt

½ teaspoon freshly ground black pepper

1 large white onion, sliced

3 cups goose or chicken white stock
   (page 209)

3 to 4 pints sauerkraut

3 cloves garlic

1 heaping tablespoon juniper berries

1 bay leaf

6 bacon slices, cut into 1-inch pieces

2 ham hocks

12 new potatoes, halved

1 carrot, peeled and sliced

2 ramps, or 1 small leek, trimmed and sliced

2 wild celery stalks or 1 domestic celery
   stalk, sliced

Preheat the oven to 375°F.

Trim a few pieces of the fat and skin from the neck and hind of the goose and set aside. Cut the goose into serving pieces. Season the goose with the salt and pepper. Heat a heavy sauté pan over medium-high heat. Add the goose fat and cook for 12 to 15 minutes, until the fat is rendered. Remove and discard the rendered pieces, leaving the fat in the pan. Add the pieces of goose and cook, turning once, for about 12 minutes on each side, until browned. Using tongs, transfer the meat to a large baking dish with a tight-fitting lid.

Add the onion to the sauté pan and cook for 5 to 7 minutes, until softened but not browned. Spread the onion on top of the goose. Discard the rendered fat or save for another use. Pour the stock over the goose.

Place the sauerkraut in a bowl and add water to cover, then drain in a colander. Press the kraut with a spoon to remove excess water. Spoon the kraut over the goose pieces. The garlic, juniper, and bay leaf will be removed after cooking, so place them in a mound in the baking dish for easy retrieval. Distribute the bacon in the dish and place the ham hocks at each end. Cover the dish and place in the oven. Cook for about 1¼ hours.

Remove the dish from the oven, uncover, and distribute the potatoes, carrot, ramps, and celery around the dish, burying them under the kraut. Cover the dish and return to the oven. Decrease the oven temperature to 350°F and cook, undisturbed, for about 1 hour. To test for doneness, slip a fork into the meat of a thigh and twist slightly. The meat should yield easily. Discard the garlic, juniper, and bay leaf.

Transfer the meat and vegetables to a serving platter and serve at once.

Growing Up in the Kitchen

"THAT'S IT! BURP THE DOUGH, LIKE A BABY."

I can still hear her words of encouragement as I pushed and pulled at the sweet bread dough with all the might my eight-year-old arms could muster. Bread making was a special event that had its beginnings in a warm yellow bowl large enough to fall into. The results were numerous, taking the form of rolls and loaves of many sizes and interesting shapes.

Lita, my beloved grandmother, was Purépecha. Although she was born in California, her people came from the state of Michoacán, in Mexico. She was a cook. Not a chef, a cook—and proud of it. I remember her best in the kitchen, where she spent most of her time. As the first born of her four granddaughters, I was called her Number One. Standing on the chair she pulled up to the counter just for me, I would "help." Together, we made bread, tamales, pies, turkey dressing, dried fruit. When we received a deer, she skinned, cleaned, and divided it into portions to be used in different dishes. My favorite was her deer jerky. With a deft hand and the help of many cracked black peppercorns, she transformed the meat into fragrant, leathery strips that we would snack on after school.

During our time in the kitchen, I learned many things. From, "Be happy when you cook or the food won't taste good," to "Always stir in one direction." I still refuse to cut lettuce or cabbage through the center, because doing so

would "break its heart." I was taught that everything had a spirit. Everything. Even a head of lettuce.

If something took a long time to simmer on the stove, so much the better. That gave us time to sit at the kitchen table and look at photo albums. Seeing pictures of my Lita with bright red lipstick and a funny hairdo—glamorous for her time—gave me a glimpse into my family history. Recounting her days as a jitterbug queen, she would treat me to impromptu dance demonstrations while the pot's contents boiled and popped in time with her energetic steps. My favorite photos were of my mother, Virginia, when she was my age. Those photographs of a brown, round face like my own promised that I too would grow up someday.

To this day, my favorite room in any home is the kitchen. It is the place where I was nourished and educated. My sisters feel this way too. When we gather, it is often around a table, sharing food we have prepared and tasting the delicious memory of a time when we were small. Lita was partial to yellow kitchens. They radiated the light and warmth of the California sun, as she did. I remember her as I lift Sophia, my niece, to her perch on the chair next to me.

—Nicolasa I. Sandoval

PHOTO COURTESY OF NICOLASA SANDOVAL

≋ From right to left: Niki Sandoval; her grandmother, Irene (Lita) Ortiz; and her sister, Carmen, ready for dinner at home in Las Vegas, 1979.

Nicolasa I. Sandoval (Chumash), an avid cook and baker, began collecting Native cookbooks during her seven-year tenure at the National Museum of the American Indian, where she served most recently as Assistant Director for Community Services. Miss Sandoval has dedicated her personal and professional life to increasing community access to artistic, cultural, and educational resources. Since 2002, she has been pursuing a doctorate in Educational Leadership and Organizations at the University of California at Santa Barbara. She resides on the Santa Ynez Indian Reservation in California.

Coos-Style Grilled Squab

||| The Coos live on the border of present-day California and Oregon, and their culture reflects both Northwest Coast and California influences. They benefit from a rich network of foods, including squab. The flavorings of huckleberry and pine needles used in this recipe are in good supply throughout the region. Domestic squab weigh about one pound, wild they weigh about ¾ pound. Squab must be cooked rare by grilling or roasting or they must be braised until very tender. There simply is no in-between for these delicious birds. While the breasts should be cooked quickly and served rare to medium, the legs must be cooked throughout. Huckleberries are in season from August through the first frost, and are available via mail order (see sources, page 215). ||| SERVES 4

4 (12- to 14-ounce) squab or pigeon

1 cup fresh huckleberries, Oregon grapes, or blackberries

2 tablespoons fresh pine needles, spruce tips, or fresh rosemary

2 small cloves garlic and 1 green onion, white part only, or 2 nodding onions, sliced

1½ tablespoons hazelnut, sunflower, or corn oil

¼ teaspoon sea or kosher salt

½ teaspoon freshly ground black pepper

To prepare the squab, run a sharp knife along both sides of the spine to remove the backbone. Use the backbone for stock or freeze it for later use. Split the birds in half and place them in a glass, ceramic, or stainless-steel pan.

Place the berries in a bowl and bruise them slightly with a fork. Pour the berries over the birds. Rinse and drain the pine needles and run a sharp knife through them once to bruise them. Sprinkle the needles over and distribute the garlic and onion among the birds. Drizzle the oil over everything and roll and turn the meat to coat evenly with the flavorings. Cover the pan and refrigerate for at least 4 hours or overnight.

Prepare a medium fire in a charcoal grill or preheat a gas grill to medium, or preheat the broiler.

Remove the birds from the marinade, letting them drain completely over the pan. Lightly scrape with a spoon to remove most of the marinade and then pat with a clean kitchen towel or paper towel, leaving the skin somewhat moist with the juices and oil. Strain the marinade, discard the solids, and reserve the liquid for basting.

Sprinkle the birds with salt and pepper and place them over indirect heat on the grill rack or in the broiler on a broiling rack. Baste with the marinade and cook for 8 to 10 minutes, until golden brown. Turn the birds over and baste again. Cook for up to 10 minutes longer, until the legs are well done and the breasts are rare, taking care not to overcook the breasts. To test for doneness, prick the joint at the leg with a fork. The juices should run clear. Transfer to a serving platter and let rest for 10 minutes before serving.

JUNIPER ROAST QUAIL WITH PIÑON NUT BUCKSKIN CAKES AND PAN GRAVY ||| This recipe was inspired by the Arizona desert, where

Tohono O'odham boys have hunted quail for centuries. Some reports suggest Gambel's quail are the most prolific type found in Arizona, although California quail seem quite common there. ||| The Wishram people of the Columbia Plateau hunted quail among the basalt draws of the present-day Deschutes and Columbia Rivers. The Yaqui of Sonora and Arizona and the Cherokee consider the bobwhite the king of quail, but all types of quail, wild or domestic, can be used to prepare this recipe. If you are using field-dressed quail (with the skin removed), wrap a piece of bacon around each bird prior to roasting. Although untraditional, a splash of Worcestershire and a sprinkle of cider vinegar open and balance the flavors of this simple gravy. Succotash, roasted squash, or roasted corn off the cob makes a nice accompaniment. ||| SERVES 4

8 (5- to 7-ounce) whole quail

1½ teaspoons juniper berries, finely chopped

Sea or kosher salt

Freshly ground black pepper

¼ cup hazelnut, sunflower, or corn oil

1 cup white stock (page 209)

1½ teaspoons masa harina, or 1 teaspoon corn starch

Dash of Tabasco sauce or other hot sauce

⅛ teaspoon ground mustard

1½ recipes Buckskin Cakes with pine nuts (page 159), made into 8 cakes

Preheat the oven to 425°F.

Wipe the quail with a damp cloth and tuck the wing tips behind the backbones. Place the quail in a roasting pan and sprinkle the rib cavities with the juniper, salt, and pepper. Place in the oven and cook for 12 to 15 minutes, depending on size, until the wings and legs are cooked through. During cooking, baste the quail every few minutes with the nut oil. Remove from the oven and keep warm.

Place the stock in a saucepan and bring to a simmer over medium heat. Place the masa in a separate saucepan over high heat and add the drippings from the quail roasting pan. Whisk together until smooth. Whisk the stock into the masa mixture and bring to a boil. Decrease the heat to medium and add the Tabasco sauce and mustard. Simmer for 10 to 15 minutes, until the masa is cooked through. Taste the gravy and add a pinch of salt or pepper if necessary. If the gravy is too thick, add a splash of stock or water.

To serve, arrange the buckskin cakes on a warm platter and place a quail on top of each cake. Spoon the gravy over the quail or pass the gravy separately. Serve immediately.

ROAST WILD TURKEY |||

Today's domestic turkeys are bred from two species indigenous to the Americas: *Meleagris gallopavo* of the eastern United States, portions of southern Canada, and northern Mexico; and *M. ocellata,* which is found in the Yucatán, Belize, and northern Guatemala. The turkey is believed to have been domesticated around 1000 B.C., somewhere in Central America. ||| Most tribes of the Americas have relished turkey for its delicious meat and for the decorative feathers of the males. Accounts dating from the Conquest record turkey as one of many magnificent game birds that graced the sophisticated table of the last Aztec king, Moctezuma. Although there is no real evidence that turkey was served at the Pilgrims' first Thanksgiving, a seventeenth-century text written by William Bradford mentions wild turkeys. In a letter sent to England, another pilgrim describes how the governor of the Plymouth Colony sent four men out fowling, and they returned with turkeys, ducks, and geese. ||| Wild tom turkeys weigh 11 to 16 pounds, and hens weigh between 6 and 10 pounds. Domestic toms weigh between 18 and 40 pounds, and hens range in weight from 8 to 10 pounds. A wild turkey is roughly half the size of a domestic turkey, with slightly smaller legs but a larger breast. The wild turkey has a more pronounced, full flavor and luscious, moist meat. Simple roasting produces the most flavorful and succulent bird, requiring little, if any, embellishment. Serve this wild turkey with roast winter squash or with roast sweet potatoes for a traditional and truly American feast. ||| Because wild turkey is deep-breasted, some cooks prefer to cover the legs and thighs with foil to prevent them from being done before the breast. The low roasting temperature in this recipe helps facilitate even browning and cooking. Still, you might prefer to tent the breast with a piece of foil to avoid overcooking it. ||| Wild turkey may be packaged with the neck bone attached and giblets packed separately. If so, cut the neck bone away from the breast, taking care not to cut the skin over the breast. Be certain to use the neck and giblets in a tasty broth by placing them in a pan with enough cold water to cover. Bring to a simmer over high heat and then decrease the heat to medium-low to a gentle simmer. Cook while the turkey is roasting and use to make gravy. ||| SERVES 6 TO 8

1 (8- to 10-pound) wild turkey hen

About ½ teaspoon sea or kosher salt

About ¼ teaspoon freshly ground black pepper

6 to 8 fresh sage leaves

¼ cup sunflower or corn oil

Preheat the oven to 375°F.

Wipe the turkey with a damp cloth. Tuck the wing tips behind the backbone. Season the cavity with salt and pepper. With a moist index finger, gently lift the skin away from each breast lobe, just enough to slip 3 or 4 sage leaves between the skin and the lobe of the breast meat. Pull the skin back into place.

Place the turkey on a roasting rack and tie the legs closed with kitchen twine. Brush the breast with the oil and place in the oven for about 30 minutes. Decrease the oven temperature to 300°F and cook, basting with the rendered pan drippings every 20 minutes, for 1½ to 2 hours. To determine if the turkey is cooked, insert the tines of a meat fork or skewer at the joint between the thigh and backbone. If the juices run very pale pink to clear and the leg and thigh give somewhat under pressure when lifted lightly with a fork, the bird is done. Let the turkey relax for at least 15 minutes before carving.

Slice into serving pieces and arrange on a platter. Serve at once.

MUSCOGEE-STYLE ROAST WILD TURKEY WITH SUNCHOKES, SWEET POTATOES, AND PECANS (MUSCOGEE PENWV [PRONOUNCED *PEN-WU*]): Omit the sage. After seasoning the breast with salt and pepper, fill the breast cavity with ½ cup diced sunchokes; 1 small unpeeled sweet potato, cut into 1-inch dice; 1 small yellow onion, cut into large dice; and ½ cup toasted and chopped pecans. Increase the cooking time to 2 to 2½ hours.

TURKEY WITH OAXACAN BLACK MOLE ||| Black moles are one of the

signature dishes of the Oaxacan region of Mexico. Here, Fernando has liberally adapted a traditional version found in

Diana Kennedy's *The Art of Mexican Cooking* using his own cooking techniques. Although untraditional, the recipe goes

well with warm Corn Tortillas (page 152), Pickled Mushrooms (page 39), or Corn and Chayote Relish (page 35) and

white rice. ||| SERVES 6 TO 8

1 (8- to 10-pound) domestic turkey hen,
    cut into 12 serving pieces

1 white onion, sliced

3 to 4 cloves garlic

1 bay leaf

1 tablespoon salt

MOLE SAUCE
1 pound tomatoes

4 dried whole pasilla chiles

4 dried whole mulato chiles

12 to 16 dried whole guajillo chiles

1/4 cup unsalted raw peanuts

1/3 cup blanched almonds

Place the turkey, onion, garlic, bay leaf, and salt in a large pot with a tight-fitting lid. Fill the pot with cold water to just cover all of the ingredients. Place the pot over high heat and bring to a rapid boil, then immediately decrease the heat to medium-low. Cover and simmer gently for 1 to 1 1/2 hours, until the turkey is tender when pierced with a fork. Using a slotted spoon, skim off the impurities as they accumulate and turn the meat with a large spoon from time to time.

While the turkey is cooking, prepare the mole sauce. Prepare a hot fire in a charcoal grill, preheat a gas grill to high, or preheat the broiler. Place the tomatoes on the grill rack or in a broiler pan and cook, turning often, for 5 to 7 minutes, until the skins are slightly blackened and blistered. Remove from the heat and allow to cool. When cool enough to handle, peel the tomatoes and transfer to a food processor or blender. Process until smooth.

Preheat the oven to 350°F. Place the pasilla, mulato, and guajillo chiles on a baking sheet and toast in the oven for 7 to 10 minutes, until soft and pliant. Do not overcook. Transfer the chiles to a cutting board. Maintain the oven temperature at 350°F. When cool enough to handle, remove and discard the chile stems. Scrape out and reserve the seeds. Place the chiles in a saucepan and cover with steaming hot tap water or boiling water. Let the chiles steep for 15 to 20 minutes.

Place the peanuts and almonds on the baking sheet and toast in the oven, stirring occasionally, for 10 to 15 minutes, until golden brown.

Place a heavy sauté pan over high heat and add the reserved chile seeds. Toast in the dry pan, stirring and tossing, for 5 to 7 minutes, until blackened. Transfer the seeds to a bowl and cover with water. Soak for 4 to 5 minutes and then pass through a fine-mesh sieve to remove the water.

¼ cup sesame seeds

3 tablespoons dried Mexican oregano or marjoram

2 whole cloves

4 whole allspice berries

1-inch piece cinnamon stick

½ cup corn oil

1 large white onion, finely chopped

2 tablespoons finely chopped garlic

1 heaping tablespoon raisins

2 ripe plantains, sliced

1 large corn tortilla, broken into pieces

2 (½-inch-thick) slices white bread, cubed

2 ounces Mexican chocolate

½ teaspoon sea or kosher salt

Drain the chiles and place in a blender with the toasted chile seeds. Process until smooth, using broth from the cooking turkey to thin the mixture if necessary. Pass the purée through a fine-mesh sieve and reserve.

Combine the sesame seeds, oregano, cloves, allspice, and cinnamon in a dry sauté pan over medium-high heat. Cook, stirring constantly, for 5 to 7 minutes, until toasted. Transfer to a spice mill and grind to a fine powder.

Heat the oil in a heavy sauté pan over medium-high heat. Add the onion and garlic and sauté for 5 to 7 minutes, until softened but not browned. Add the tomato purée and cook, stirring often, for about 5 minutes. Add the peanuts, almonds, spice powder, raisins, and plantains. Decrease the heat to medium and cook, stirring often, for about 15 minutes. In small batches, transfer to a blender and process to a smooth, thick sauce, using broth from the cooking turkey to thin the mixture if necessary.

Return the tomato purée to the sauté pan over medium heat. Add the chile purée, tortilla, bread, chocolate, salt, and 4 to 5 cups of the broth from the cooking turkey. Simmer, stirring more often now to keep the sauce from sticking, for about 30 minutes, to make a thick, pourable sauce. Adjust the consistency with additional turkey broth if necessary. Remove from the heat and allow to cool slightly. With an immersion blender or in very small batches in a blender, purée until very smooth. The finished sauce should be thick enough to richly coat the pieces of the turkey. Taste and adjust the seasoning with salt if necessary. Return the sauce to a large sauté pan over medium heat.

Using a slotted spoon, transfer the turkey pieces to the sauce in the pan. Warm through for about 15 minutes, adjusting the consistency of the sauce by increasing the heat to high and reducing if it is too thin or adding broth if it is too thick. Transfer the turkey and sauce to a serving dish, passing extra sauce on the side. Serve immediately.

CHICKEN WITH BLACK MOLE: Replace the turkey with 1 (3- to 4-pound) stewing hen, cut into pieces. Decrease the initial cooking time to 45 to 60 minutes. There will be enough sauce to prepare twice this amount of chicken. The sauce freezes well when covered tightly and frozen. Serves 4.

ROAST WILD DUCK WITH JUNIPER AND WILD PLUM

SAUCE ||| While this is a nontraditional recipe, it was developed with respect for both custom and common

sense. Duck breasts should be cooked rare. Hindquarters are best cooked thoroughly. Cooks for centuries have developed ways to use all parts of their hard-earned quarry. Early American hunters would have wanted to eat the meat at its finest and undoubtedly understood that it was best to retrieve the breasts when the skin was crisped and to allow the legs to continue cooking over the fire. Serve with Wild Rice and Corn Fritters (page 14) and watercress dressed with Hazelnut Vinaigrette (page 49). ||| SERVES 4

2 (1- to 1½ pound) wild Muscovy or
   mallard ducks, or 2 (2- to 3-pound)
   domestic ducks

Sea or kosher salt

Freshly ground black pepper

8 juniper berries, bruised and chopped

2 bay leaves

4 ramps, trimmed and sliced, or 2 cloves
   garlic and 2 green onions, sliced

2 teaspoons tomato paste

½ cup wild plums, huckleberries, wild
   cherries, or domestic tart dried cherries,
   pitted

6 cups chicken or duck white stock
   (page 209)

Preheat the oven to 550°F.

Pat the ducks with a moist cloth to remove any blood or moisture. Cut off the wing tips and necks, placing them (along with gizzards and hearts, if you have them) in a roasting pan. Sprinkle salt and pepper inside the cavities and on the outside of each duck. Divide the juniper and bay leaves and place in the cavities of each duck. Tie the legs closed with kitchen twine. Lay the ducks on their sides over the trimmed pieces in the roasting pan. Place the pan in the oven and roast for 7 minutes. Turn the ducks to the other side and roast for 7 minutes. Turn the breasts to face up and roast for about 12 minutes. To test for doneness, prick the thigh with a fork. The juices should run clear. Remove from the oven and transfer the ducks to a platter. Tent with aluminum foil and keep warm.

Pour off and discard the fat from the roasting pan. Transfer the necks and wing tips to a saucepan over medium-high heat, scraping in any meat glazes that developed from roasting. Add the ramps and cook, stirring constantly, for 7 to 8 minutes, until the ramps are browned. Add the tomato paste and plums and stir well. Add the stock and cook, stirring occasionally, until the mixture comes to a full boil. Decrease the heat to medium to achieve a slow boil. Using a slotted spoon, skim off any impurities as they accumulate. Cook the sauce for about 20 minutes, until reduced by two-thirds.

While the sauce is cooking, section the ducks. Cut along both sides of the backbone and remove it. Put the backs in the saucepan with the sauce. Lay the ducks on the cutting board and cut between the breast and hindquarter to remove the thigh and leg. Cover the ducks again with the foil.

Pass the sauce through a fine-mesh sieve into a clean saucepan and discard the bones and flavorings. Return the sauce to the stove over medium heat and bring to a gentle simmer. Skim off any impurities as they accumulate. Continue to simmer gently while browning the duck.

Preheat the broiler. Place the duck hindquarters on a broiler pan and sprinkle with salt. Place in the broiler for 10 to 12 minutes, until crisp and golden brown. Transfer to a warm serving platter. Place the duck breasts on the broiler pan and broil for 2 to 3 minutes, until crisp and golden brown. Transfer to the serving platter. Serve immediately, passing the sauce on the side.

≋ A diorite bowl carved with the figure of a monstrous, bird-headed serpent. A.D. 1250–1500. Alabama. (16/5232)

CHAPTER SIX

FOODS FROM RIVERS, LAKES, & OCEANS

≈ Rappahanock men hauling fish nets, 1918. Chickahominy River, Virginia. (N12638)

Depictions of fish harvests survive in petroglyphs and pictographs etched and painted thousands of years ago by indigenous peoples throughout the Western Hemisphere. After contact with Native cultures, Europeans recorded with pen, paper, canvas, and paint the significance of fishing for the peoples they encountered. Along with these early Contact illustrations, rock pictures reveal the sophisticated practices of indigenous fishermen throughout the Americas. Prehistoric fish weirs were used to harvest all types of fish along the shorelines and rivers of North and South America and Hawai'i. A network of causeways led to the fish weirs and ponds of the Baure of the Bolivian Amazon region. The Calusa people, who lived in the region that is now Florida, created a vast system of fenced lagoons for cultivating oysters and clams. In Hawai'i, both freshwater ponds and coastal inlets were used for a type of early aquaculture, where attendants raised fish, shellfish, and sea vegetables for royalty.

The origins of many modern fishing methods can be traced directly or indirectly to the early inhabitants of the Americas. Their countless types of hooks, rigging, nets, weirs, traps, and other fishing and aquaculture practices were communicated to the Europeans through the distinct vocabularies of different Native groups.

The Wampanoag of Massachusetts had a broad-based vocabulary for a lifestyle based on water. For example, *hoquaún* meant a hook—any hook. Small hooks, *peewâsicks,* and big hooks, *maúmacocks,* required further elaboration. Like many indigenous peoples, the Wampanoag had specific words for types of fish that were of daily or regular importance, while other, less common types were described by a general term.

The Ojibwe and Potawatomi of the Great Lakes region fished with a line and a hook fashioned from deer bone or native copper. Fish traps were constructed from twigs and tree branches to catch sturgeon and smaller fish. Sturgeon was prized for its roe (caviar) and was eaten fresh or dried.

The Hidatsa people, who lived along the Missouri River, were not as dependent on fishing as the coastal tribes, but fish—usually catfish—did form a part of their diet. Their main technique for catching fish was the fish trap, made by certain men who had purchased the sacred right to make traps. The traps were usually composed of willow mats attached to willow poles stuck into the mud in a shallow area of the river. Bait was attached to the gate to attract the fish. Branches with leaves were put near the trap, and when the leaves shook, the trap was full and the gate closed. The fisherman would then scoop out the fish with cone-shaped willow baskets.

Peoples of North and South America continue to practice diverse and traditional methods of harvesting fish. The Inuit people of Canada and Alaska still lie on ice floes in shallow water and jig for salmon, halibut, and arctic char. When the fish are attracted to the lure, the fishermen spear them with a type of trident.

One means of salmon fishing used in the Columbia Plateau region of North America required building wooden platforms that projected over the rushing waters to facilitate the snaring of salmon as they made their way upstream. This early method is still widely used today by the peoples of that region. The availability of fish, salmon in particular, influenced whether or not Northwest Coast people thrived. Many families continue to return to their fishing camps for fall and spring harvests. Like their ancestors, their goal is to harvest and preserve enough fish to carry them through the winter.

Shrimp, crab, or lobster boiled in fresh seawater; fresh-caught trout, cornmeal-dipped and pan-fried on the spot; fresh oysters on the half-shell, swallowed minutes after being raised from the beach—there simply are no better ways to eat fish and shellfish. This is how our elders consumed their first catch, with reverence and much gratitude. The balance was preserved for later use. The recipes that follow reflect the simple ways Native peoples prepare such foods, beyond the powerfully gratifying moment of the first catch.

PHOTO BY LOMEN BROTHERS STUDIO

≋ Bering Strait Inuit hunters, circa 1912. (N35421)

GREAT LAKES PIKE WITH MAPLE GLAZE ||| The Dakota word for

maple syrup is *cha-n ha-n pi,* or "wood tree juice." Dark maple syrup blended with nut oil and a little juniper gives this delectable fish a lovely, deep amber glaze. If maple leaves are unavailable, leek tops, banana leaves, or salicornia can be substituted. Serve this fish with a simple succotash of corn or hominy, with northern beans flavored with onions and a little bacon, or with wild rice. ||| SERVES 2

1/4 cup pure maple syrup

2 tablespoons walnut oil

Pinch of sea or kosher salt

Pinch of freshly ground black pepper

2 juniper berries, crushed and finely
  chopped

4 to 6 green maple leaves, moistened

1 (2 1/2-pound) northern pike or walleye,
  filleted and skinned

Prepare a large fire in a charcoal grill or preheat a gas grill to medium-high. Allow the charcoal to burn down to glowing embers. Place 1 pound of maple branches or soaked maple wood chips over the embers.

In a bowl, combine the syrup, oil, salt, pepper, and juniper and mix well.

Place the maple leaves on the grill rack away from the center of the heat and lay the fish on the leaves. Baste the fillets with the syrup mixture. Cover the grill and cook for about 2 minutes. Baste again, cover the grill, and cook for about 2 minutes more. Baste again to use up the glaze, cover the grill, and cook for 4 to 8 minutes, until the fillets are opaque and moist.

Transfer to a serving platter and serve at once.

BASIC CURED FISH |||

Methods of fish preservation among Native peoples are diverse throughout the Americas. In North America, numerous techniques date to prehistoric times. The Delaware dried their fish by fire, as did the Innu of Canada's St. Lawrence River region. Sun-drying was widely used, from the Pueblo tribes of New Mexico to the Montauk of New York to the Pomo of California. Smoke alone was used to preserve the catches of the Mississippi Natchez and the Coast Salish in British Columbia, while a combination of smoke and sun-drying was used by the Narragansett and Huron in the Northeast. The Ojibwe of the Great Lakes and the Quechua of South America's Pacific Coast practiced drying, smoking, and freezing. The Yuchi of southeastern North America combined salting and drying to preserve their fish. ||| With time being an important concern for most modern home cooks, preservation of fish is more likely to be relegated to a professional. However, the flavors of smoked and preserved foods are as desirable today as they were a benefit of necessity in the past. A few traditional and nontraditional techniques have been adapted and modified here so that you can enjoy these great flavors at home. The basic recipe works for salmon, arctic char, cutthroat trout, kokanee, and halibut. The fish may cure for about six hours. Then it is rinsed, smoked (see page 203), or cured for three days. After this process, it can be sliced and eaten as is. Serve with Buckskin Cakes (page 159), poached quail eggs, and watercress. ||| MAKES ABOUT 2 POUNDS

2 pounds fish fillets or whole sides of smaller fish, such as salmon, arctic char, cutthroat trout, kokanee, or halibut, skin on

½ cup sea or kosher salt (do not use table salt)

½ cup honey, pure maple syrup, or sugar

Remove any bones from the fish fillets. Place the fish skin side down in a nonreactive container (earthenware, ceramic, stainless steel, or glass).

To make the cure, combine the salt and honey in a bowl and mix thoroughly with a metal spoon. Generously spread the mixture over the fillets and, using the back of the spoon or your hands, rub it lightly into the meat. Cover the fish with plastic wrap and place a weight (a clean board, brick, or a rectangular casserole dish works well) over the fillets. Cover and refrigerate for at least 3 days. Turn the fillets several times throughout the curing process.

To serve the cured fish, remove the fish from the brine, rinse with cool water, and pat dry. Lay the fish on a cutting board and, using a very sharp knife with a thin, straight blade, slice the fish at an angle. Leaving the skin intact helps greatly in this process.

CHIMAKUM CURE: After rubbing the fish with the basic cure, sprinkle the fillets evenly with 1 tablespoon minced wild or cultivated fresh mint, ¼ cup peeled and minced licorice fern root (or 1 cup minced fennel tops), and 1 tablespoon mustard seed.

PINE CURE: After rubbing the fish with the basic cure, sprinkle the fillets evenly with 1 cup soaked, drained, and minced ponderosa, lodgepole, or western white pine needles; 1 tablespoon finely chopped juniper berries; and 1 tablespoon freshly ground black pepper.

≋ Harvesting salt from la Laguna del Rosario, Oaxaca, 2001. (E121)

SMOKED HERRING ||| Various Northwest tribes, such as the Skokomish near Mt. Vernon, Washington, prepared a version of smoked herring. Fresh herring, like all small fish, can be boned by applying gentle downward pressure on both sides of the backbone with your thumb from the neck to the tail following the spine. Grab the spine at the neck and pull downward to remove it. Serve with Toasted Filbert Cakes (page 160) and a light salad. ||| SERVES 4

2 pounds herring, skin on (4 to 6 fish)

1/2 cup sea or kosher salt (do not use table salt)

1/2 cup honey, pure maple syrup, or sugar

Remove the herring entrails, rinse the fish, and pat dry. Place the fish in a nonreactive container (earthenware, ceramic, stainless, or glass).

To make the cure, combine the salt and honey in a bowl and mix thoroughly with a metal spoon. Generously spread the mixture over the fish and, using the back of the spoon or your hands, rub it lightly into the cavity of the fish. Cover the fish with plastic wrap and refrigerate for at least 24 hours. Turn the fish several times throughout the curing process.

Remove the fish from the brine, rinse with cool water, and pat dry. Place on a rack over a drip tray and let the fish dry overnight, uncovered, in the refrigerator.

To smoke the herring, prepare the smoker with the fuel and set the temperature to about 160° F. Place the herring on the smoker racks and place in the smoker. Smoke for 2 to 3 hours, until the internal temperature of the herring reaches 160° F when a probe thermometer is inserted and the flesh is opaque and moist. Transfer to plates and serve at once.

≈ A nineteenth-century Haida carved sheephorn bowl. Sheephorn bowls were usually filled with oil or grease rendered from seal or whale blubber or from the highly prized eulachon (candlefish). Guests dip chunks of dried salmon, potatoes, and other foods into the grease to add richness and flavor. (9/8059)

LAWALU SNAPPER |||

Among the fish favored for this traditional Hawaiian preparation are *ehu* (short-tailed red snapper), *onaga* (long-tailed red snapper), and *'ama 'ama* (striped mullet). *'Ama 'ama* was traditionally pond-raised. Some ancient fish ponds are now being restored through aquaculture not only to produce fish but also to reintroduce an early practice. All of these fish are suitable for this recipe, and American red snapper or any fish with large, flaky fillets can be substituted. The term *lawalu* refers to fish or meat that is wrapped in ti or banana leaves and steamed. Ti leaves can be found at Asian markets. ||| SERVES 4

2 large banana leaves, or 4 ti leaves

4 (8-ounce) fillets snapper, skin on

¼ cup coconut or palm oil

1 teaspoon Hawaiian, sea, or kosher salt

2 tablespoons tamari or low-sodium soy sauce

4 coin-sized slices peeled fresh ginger

2 cloves garlic, halved

2 tablespoons sesame oil

2 pounds laver, dulse, or kelp seaweed, or salicornia or leek tops

Prepare a large fire in a charcoal grill or preheat a gas grill to medium-high. Allow the charcoal to burn down to glowing embers. Place 1 pound of kiawe wood chips, or any wood suitable for smoking, over the embers.

Cut each banana leaf into 2 equal pieces. Lay each fillet skin-side down on a piece of leaf. Rub the fillets with the coconut oil and sprinkle with salt. Evenly drizzle the tamari over the fillets. Tuck 1 piece of the ginger and 1 piece of the garlic under each fillet between the skin and the leaf. Sprinkle the sesame oil over the fillets and wrap each one by folding the banana leaf over the top.

Distribute half of the seaweed over the coals and wood chips. Lay the fish bundles seam side down on the seaweed and cover with the remaining seaweed. Cover the grill and steam for 8 to 10 minutes. To check for doneness, insert the tip of a knife into the fish. If the knife emerges warm to hot to the touch, the fish is cooked. Transfer the fish bundles to a warm serving tray and serve at once.

Catfish Stew with Succotash ||| The Hidatsa are thought to have

made a similar stew. The appealing flavors make this a dish that has withstood the test of time. You can still find variations of it throughout the upper Midwest. Serve with warm cornbread or Buckskin Cakes (page 159). ||| SERVES 4

1 cup northern beans

½ teaspoon sea or kosher salt

2 bacon slices, chopped

1 small white onion, sliced

2 catfish (about 1½ pounds), skinned and
    cut into 2-inch pieces

1 bay leaf

1 (13-ounce) can white hominy, drained

3 to 4 wapato, sunchokes, or new potatoes,
    peeled and sliced ¼ inch thick

3 cups chicken or fish white stock (page 209)

Freshly ground black pepper

Rinse the beans in 2 changes of cold water. Place the beans in a saucepan and add water to cover. Cover, place over high heat, and bring to a boil. Remove from the heat and let steep for 1 hour. Place over high heat and bring to a boil. Decrease the heat to medium-low, add the salt, and cook for about 1½ hours, until tender. Drain well.

Heat a heavy soup pot over medium-high heat. Add the bacon and cook, stirring occasionally, for 3 to 5 minutes, until the fat is rendered. Add the onion and cook for 2 minutes, without browning. Add the beans, catfish, bay leaf, hominy, wapato, and stock, and a pinch of salt and pepper. Bring to a slow boil and then decrease the heat to low. Gently simmer the stew for 10 to 15 minutes, until the fish is cooked through. Remove the fish with a slotted spoon and keep warm.

Increase the heat to medium-high and cook for 5 to 7 minutes, until the liquid is reduced to just cover the beans and the wapato is tender. Ladle the succotash into warmed soup bowls. Divide the fish among the bowls and serve at once.

SALMON COOKERY

THOUSANDS OF YEARS OF CULINARY EVOLUTION have shaped the way salmon is cooked today by Northwest Coast peoples. Long winters were devoted to preparing for the spring and summer harvesting season, when the salmon would make their annual return to the waters of the people. Special implements for preparing salmon were fashioned from seashells, abundant local woods, or stones. Today in the Pacific Northwest, rack barbecues and modern smokers most often replace more traditional smoking methods.

The size and variety of the salmon directly influence the way the fish is prepared. Pieces from a large Chinook salmon can be positioned on spits over a fire built to accommodate a single-pole rack. Smaller coho or sockeye salmon, weighing up to 6 pounds, may be cooked whole on a spit-pole device. Whole fish may be cooked on a spit pole made of sapling strapping over a pit fire or over a fire with a rack fashioned like a grill. All sizes of fish may be smoked over a small smoldering fire made of wet and green wood, usually alder, to produce low heat and lots of smoke.

The imu method of the Coast Salish produces especially tantalizing results. Traditionally, an imu fire pit is dug and then filled with smooth lava rocks. A fire is then built over the rocks. Whole salmon is wrapped with ocean spray leaves or fern leaves. When the fire burns low, it is raked aside. Seaweed is then placed over the hot rocks, followed by the leaf-wrapped salmon and other foods to accompany the salmon (such as camas root, potatoes, and shellfish). A final layer of seaweed is placed on top. The entire package of food is then buried with the coals of the fire, additional hot rocks and gravel, and left to cook. An hour is allowed to cook the first ten pounds of salmon, with ten more minutes for each additional pound.

PHOTO BY LARRY McNEIL

≈ A resident of the village of Angoon in southeast Alaska fillets some sockeye salmon that will be smoked. Many Alaska Natives continue to hunt and fish for subsistence. (P26515)

Imu-Style Salmon ||| The coastal peoples of the Pacific Northwest employed leaf- or seaweed-wrapped pit cookery, as did many others, including the Hawaiian, Maya, Inka, and Aztec cultures. Some form of pit cookery was also common to the people of the Iroquois Confederacy, the Great Lakes region, the Mississippian cultures, and the southern coast of North America. This imu-style salmon recipe and its variants, the lawalu-wrapped fish of Hawai'i (page 127), and the Maya-Style Steamed Fish with Achiote (page 133), will provide some fine examples. ||| Using salicornia (a sea bean) and sea salt reproduces the effect of seawater, maximizing the flavor and texture of this simple but extraordinary-tasting dish. Serve with crusty bread and a simple salad dressed with nut oil and lemon juice. Try substituting trout for the salmon for a nice variation. ||| SERVES 4

1 pound laver, dulse, or kelp seaweed,
  or salicornia or leek tops

4 (6-ounce) fillets salmon or steelhead

1 tablespoon corn oil

1 teaspoon sea or kosher salt

1/4 cup salmon caviar

1/4 cup hazelnut or walnut oil

Prepare a large fire in a charcoal grill or preheat a gas grill to medium-high. Allow the charcoal to burn down to glowing embers. Place 1 pound alder wood chips, or any wood suitable for smoking, over the embers.

Spread half of the seaweed in a slight mound to one side of the grill, over indirect heat. Rub the fillets with the corn oil and sprinkle with the salt. Place the fish on the seaweed and cover with the remaining seaweed. Cover the grill and smoke for 10 to 15 minutes, until the salmon is cooked through, taking care not to overcook.

To serve, place a small mound of the seaweed on each dinner plate. Place the fish on the seaweed, top with the salmon caviar, and drizzle with the nut oil. Serve immediately.

HONORING THE SALMON

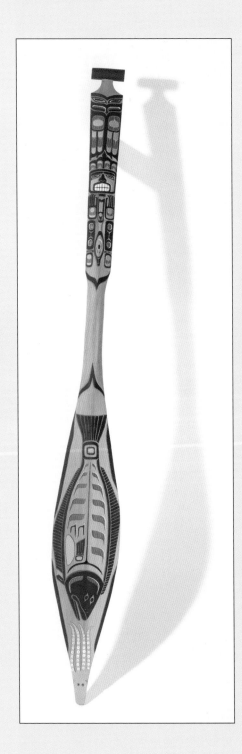

INDIGENOUS PEOPLE OF THE AMERICAS often center their religious beliefs on the bounties from the land and water. Salmon were once abundant in the waters of both North and South America. The remarkable life cycle of salmon—hatching, growing, traveling to sea, and returning years later to the same spot to lay its eggs—conveyed a significant message to indigenous people. They too believed their homeland was where they belonged, no matter how far they roamed for hunting, gathering, or trading. For many of the Northwest Coast's Native people, salmon remains not only a source of food but also a source of spiritual connection to land and water.

When the salmon return to spawn in fresh waters throughout the region, it is a cause for widespread ceremonies that give thanks to the Creator. The first salmon caught in the spring is always treated with great dignity and receives a special ceremony celebrating its arrival. Lummi children sing the "Salmon Song." The villagers join in the "Welcome Song" while an elder *siem*, or leader, gives thanks.

The welcome prayers of different tribes are surprisingly similar to each other. In her book *Indian Fishing*, Hilary Stewart transcribes a song that bears a striking resemblance to this one from a fisherman in northern waters:

> *Haya, Haya!*
> *Rise again, Swimmer, we have met in good health.*
> *Welcome, Supernatural One, you are a long-life-maker,*
>   *you come to see me*
> *once again as you always do.*
> *Now I pray take my sickness back to your rich country on the*
> *far side of the world, Supernatural One.*

≈ Wood paddle representing fish, bear mask, bear paw, and octopus, by Bill Martin (Makah), 1992. Neah Bay, Washington. (T25/3355)

MAYA-STYLE STEAMED FISH WITH ACHIOTE ||| Like the

Yucatán-Style Pork (page 89), this is an adaptation of a traditional pit cookery preparation. Cooking this dish over a slow-burning barbecue fitted with a tightly sealed cover produces excellent results. Serve with Pickled Red Onions (page 40), tortillas, steamed rice, and black beans. ||| SERVES 4

2 pounds fresh dorado (mahi mahi) or
   American red snapper fillets, skin on

2 tablespoons achiote paste

2 cloves garlic, minced

Juice of 1 lime

Juice of 1 orange

Juice of 1 grapefruit

1 teaspoon sea or kosher salt

1 banana leaf, for cooking

¼ cup corn oil

Cut the fish into 4 pieces. In a bowl, combine the achiote paste, garlic, and citrus juices and mix until completely blended. Add the fish and sprinkle with the salt. Toss until the fish is completely coated.

Preheat the oven to 375°F.

Line a baking sheet with the banana leaf, providing generous overhang. Place the fish on the leaf and pour any remaining seasoning paste over the top. Drizzle the oil over the fish and fold the banana leaf over the fish to completely cover. Tuck the leaf under the fish to secure. Cover the baking sheet with aluminum foil.

Place in the oven and bake for about 35 minutes, until the fish flakes when gently pierced with a fork. Remove from the oven. Using a spatula, transfer the fish package to a serving platter. Pour the accumulated liquid into a gravy dish and pass separately with the fish.

CEVICHE DE ECUADOR ||| The people of Ecuador serve ceviche as a meal with fresh salted popcorn and toasted corn that resembles North America's corn nuts. Some Ecuadorans cook the fish slightly before marinating it, but a silken, firm texture is achieved when the fish is "cooked" in the marinade. ||| SERVES 4 TO 6

¼ cup freshly squeezed lemon juice

2 tablespoons corn oil

½ small red onion, finely chopped

½ small red bell pepper, finely chopped

1 celery stalk, finely chopped

1 small hot chile, seeded and finely chopped

1 pound fresh sea bass fillets, skinned and
    cut into ½-inch cubes

2 tablespoons minced cilantro

Sea or kosher salt

Freshly ground black pepper

In a large bowl, combine the lemon juice, oil, onion, bell pepper, celery, and chile and mix well. Add the fish and toss to coat evenly. Cover and refrigerate for about 4 hours to "cook" the fish and develop the flavors.

To serve, divide among salad plates and sprinkle with the cilantro, salt, and pepper.

PERUVIAN CEBICHE

||| Through a melding of Old and New World traditions, Central and South American people now claim cebiche, or ceviche, as one of their most commonly shared dishes. One way to serve this cebiche is to fill ripe avocado halves with it and serve in bowls with plenty of the flavorful liquid spooned over the fish. Cebiche is also a popular appetizer. ||| SERVES 4 TO 6

Juice of 1 orange

Juice of 1 lemon

Juice of 2 limes

1/2 cup tomato juice

1/8 teaspoon sea or kosher salt

Pinch of freshly ground black pepper

1 pound fresh skinned sea bass, scallops, or squid, or a combination of all three

1 small tomato

1/2 small red onion, coarsely chopped

1/2 cup chopped cilantro

1/4 cup peanut oil

1 hot red chile, seeded and finely chopped

1/2 red bell pepper, coarsely chopped

In a large bowl, combine the citrus juices, tomato juice, salt, and pepper and mix well. Cut the fish into bite-sized pieces and add to the marinade. Toss to coat evenly. Cover and refrigerate for about 4 hours.

Prepare a hot fire in a charcoal grill, preheat a gas grill to high, or preheat the broiler. Place the tomato on the grill rack or in a broiler pan and cook, turning often, for 4 to 5 minutes, until the skin is slightly blackened and blistered. Peel the tomato and chop coarsely. Allow to cool completely.

To serve, add the tomato, onion, cilantro, oil, chile, and bell pepper to the fish and toss to coat evenly. Let stand at room temperature for at least 30 minutes and up to 2 hours prior to serving.

Serve the fish in clear glass dishes accompanied by the marinade.

COAST SALISH—STYLE MUSSELS

||| Although this dish is prepared by peoples of the Oregon coast, it could easily be made by any coast culture. The Mi'kmaq use seawater alone to flavor and cook the mussels. The Kwakiutl and Yaki use dulse, a type of seaweed. Use whatever is fresh and in season in your area. Don't limit this recipe to mussels if you have other shellfish available. Clams, quahogs, shrimp, crab, and even lobster would work. Fish can be prepared in this manner as well, but use whole fish or steaks. Seafood is always best when bought locally and fresh, and when flavored with ingredients that are grown in your area. A crusty loaf of bread and a salad to accompany this simple dish will make a satisfying lunch or light supper. ||| SERVES 4

2 tablespoons corn oil

6 wild onions, or 1 large leek, chopped

½ cup chicken white stock (page 209)
    or water

½ cup water

3 pounds mussels, scrubbed and debearded

½ pound salicornia or leek tops

1 lemon, cut into 4 thick slices

¼ cup unsalted butter

Sea salt

Freshly ground black pepper

Heat the oil in a pan with a tight-fitting lid over medium-high heat. Add the onions and cook for 1 to 2 minutes, until softened but not browned. Add the stock, water, and mussels. Distribute the salicornia over the mussels and cover the pan. Cook for 8 to 10 minutes, until the mussels open and are just cooked through. Discard any mussels that do not open. Squeeze the lemon over the mussels, and then drop the slices into the pan. Add the butter and season to taste with salt and pepper. Simmer until the butter is melted. Serve the mussels in bowls with the broth and salicornia.

CHILLED GULF SHRIMP IN CHIPOTLE SAUCE ||| This modern

version of an Aztec dish calls for prodigious amounts of chipotle chiles, which makes the shrimp hot and smoky.

Sample the heat intensity by tasting a tiny bit of the sauce. You may prefer to use fewer chiles to suit your taste. Serve the

shrimp with crisp corn tortillas and slices of ripe papaya and avocado. ||| SERVES 4

2 tomatoes

1 pound Mexican shrimp (16 count), peeled
    and deveined

1/4 cup freshly squeezed lime juice

Sea or kosher salt

1 teaspoon Mexican oregano or marjoram

1/4 cup corn oil

1/4 white onion, thinly sliced

4 chipotle chiles en adobo

2 small cloves garlic

1/4 cup dry white wine (optional)

Prepare a hot fire in a charcoal grill, preheat a gas grill to high, or pre-heat the broiler. Place the tomatoes on the grill rack or in a broiler pan and cook, turning often, for 4 to 5 minutes, until the skins are slightly black-ened and blistered. When cool enough to handle, peel the tomatoes.

Place the shrimp and lime juice in a bowl. Sprinkle with salt, cover, and refrigerate for 10 to 15 minutes.

Heat a small sauté pan over medium heat. Add the oregano and cook, stirring constantly, for 5 to 7 minutes, until toasted.

Heat the oil in a heavy sauté pan over medium-high heat. Add the onion and cook for 3 minutes, until softened but not browned.

Drain the shrimp and reserve the marinade. Add the shrimp to the onion and cook for 3 to 5 minutes, until the shrimp are about half-cooked. With a slotted spoon, transfer the shrimp and onion to a bowl. Reserve the oil in the pan.

Combine the tomatoes, chiles, and garlic in the bowl of a food proces-sor. Process until the mixture resembles coarse meal. Heat the sauté pan with the reserved oil over medium-high heat. Add the tomato mixture and cook for about 8 minutes, stirring often and turning the pan to prevent the sauce from sticking or burning. Add the oregano, reserved marinade, and wine. Bring to a boil and add the shrimp and onion. Cook for about 2 min-utes, just long enough to flavor the shrimp, and remove from the heat when the shrimp are just slightly underdone, to allow for residual cooking time.

With a slotted spoon, remove the shrimp from the sauce and place in a bowl. Cover the shrimp loosely and place in the refrigerator to chill. Pour the sauce into a separate bowl, cover loosely, and immediately refrigerate for at least 1 hour. Serve the shrimp well chilled with the sauce alongside.

DUNGENESS CRAB HASH ||| This is the perfect dish for leftovers from crab feeds and

fish feasts with friends and families. Though this recipe is untraditional, it combines some New World ingredients for a delicious breakfast alternative. Use any leftover fish or shellfish in place of the crab. Serve with poached eggs on top for a real treat. ||| SERVES 4

2 russet or other starchy potatoes

Zest of 1 lemon

2 tablespoons unsalted butter

2 tablespoons corn oil

½ small leek, white part only, finely sliced

2 tablespoons finely chopped white onion

2 tablespoons minced red bell pepper

12 ounces crabmeat (about 1½ cups), picked over for shells

1 tablespoon minced fresh dill

Sea salt

Freshly ground black pepper

Preheat the oven to 400°F. Place the potatoes on the oven rack and bake for about 45 minutes, until fork-tender. Remove from the oven and allow to cool. When cool enough to handle, grate the potatoes.

Place the zest in a small saucepan with water to cover. Place over high heat and bring to a boil. Drain and repeat the process 2 more times. Rinse the zest with cold water, pat dry, and chop.

Melt the butter in a cast-iron skillet over medium-high heat. Add the oil and heat through. Add the potatoes, spread out evenly, and cook for 5 to 7 minutes without disturbing. Spread the leek, onion, and bell pepper on top of the potatoes and cook for 5 to 7 minutes, until the bottom is golden brown. Spread the crabmeat on top and sprinkle with the zest, dill, and salt and pepper to taste. Turn the entire cake over with a spatula and cook for 7 minutes, or until the hash is heated throughout and crisp. Serve immediately.

SMOKED SALMON HASH: Replace the crab with 12 ounces flaked smoked salmon.

People of the Salmon

NUSUXMÍ TANÁNMA

PARTICIPATING IN A RECENT TASTE TEST of wild salmon in our offices at Ecotrust in Portland, Oregon, reminds me of a time when salmon ran plentifully, and I took them for granted. In the community of Warm Springs, Oregon, where I ate most of my salmon as a child in the 1960s, declines in salmon populations had yet to be noticed. The industrious women prepared the fish with good thoughts, laughter, and prayers, so it always tasted good.

During the summer, when our fishers had abundant catches, we barbecued the fresh salmon. Tethered to sticks over an open fire, tended by a patient cook, its fat dripping and shushing, the gorgeous orange flesh turned from a dark to a lighter shade of coral, and the skin on the side closest to the heat curled and browned. Of course, we were outside, and the scent of smoke mingled with the serene smells of earth, trees, and water.

For many tribes of the Northwest, the longhouse is a gathering place of spiritual well-being. The door faces east, and the drummers sit on the northern side. Old longhouses had dirt floors for our feet to touch earth and a smoke hole that carried our songs and prayers to the Creator. In our First Fruits ceremonies, we collectively honor and thank the food for returning each season. In the longhouse at Warm Springs, we take one of the four sacred foods in our mouths at the start of a First Fruits ceremonial meal. At the end of the meal, we sip water to celebrate and recognize all of the life that enriches us.

For our community at Warm Springs, and for others along the Columbia River Plateau, salmon is one of the four sacred foods. These four gifts—salmon, venison, roots, and berries—sustain our body, spirit, and culture. Great quantities and varieties of these foods are served during our longhouse feasts. Sometimes only the head and tails of the salmon are offered.

Fish cheeks are a delicacy, which we reserve for the elders. Our elders need these Indian foods. Without wild foods they would weaken and die. My great-aunt joked about the quick energy bars sold in stores as she handed me a *Looksh-me,* a dried root in cookie form. "Here's some power food for you," she said. The sweet taste of Looksh-me is a perfect complement to pieces of air-dried salmon, what most call jerky. You don't need much of these power foods—you could go for a long time with both stashed in your travel bag, along with some good water.

I like my salmon wild and straight, with no frills or additional flavorings except those transmitted by the fire. The firm and healthy fish flakes right off in layers; you don't even need a fork. In the cold winter months, when you feel yourself catching a bug, chew a few strips of Columbia River Plateau–style salmon jerky. This means it has been dried in the hot wind that comes over the yellow hills and blows past the volcanic basalt columns that rim our river canyons. The pure oils and the texture of the flesh as it spreads over your taste buds is an exotic treat, since fresh Native foods are difficult to find in the winter. The moment it hits your system, you feel warm inside, like a high-desert summer. All the minerals and essential oils you need are there in one good source.

I took all this for granted in childhood. Blessed with many varieties of salmon, I took only as much as I needed, not in the interests of ecological preservation but rather as way of respecting and observing my maternal family's culture. My great-great-great-grandmother, Kah-Nee-Ta, taught my grandmother to catch only what was needed and to let the rest go. Today, the vanishing of our traditional salmon runs parallels the disappearance of our Native languages. We understand less with each loss. To preserve this precious link between culture and environment, eat non-farmed, wild salmon and buy from Native foods producers. This helps boost the natural systems as well as the indigenous peoples whose livelihood depends on the survival and diversity of the great salmon.

—Elizabeth Woody

Elizabeth Woody (Navajo/Warm Springs/Wasco/Yakama) is the author of three books of poetry and short prose pieces. Her first collection of poetry, *Hand into Stone,* received the American Book Award. Among other honors, she also has received a J. T. Stewart Fellowship from Hedgebrook and a William Stafford Memorial Award for Poetry from the Pacific Northwest Bookseller's Association. She is the director of the Indigenous Leadership Program for Ecotrust in Portland, Oregon.

For more information about wild salmon and Native foods organizations, visit www.salmonnation.com.

≋ **Emily Charles checking salmon hung over a fire. Celilo Falls, Oregon, circa 1950.**

PAN-FRIED FROG LEGS ||| Tribes in the Plains and Great Lakes regions were cooking

frog legs long before contact with Europeans. In its flavorings, this recipe reveals Scandinavian influence on a tradi-

tional preparation. Some folks like to soak frog legs overnight in lemon, vinegar, and ice, or even in milk, to tenderize

them, but you still get excellent results by simply cleaning and cooking them. Serve with lemon wedges and steamed

wild rice or over fried potatoes or wapato. ||| SERVES 4

8 pairs frog legs, skinned, cleaned,
    and rinsed

Juice of 2 lemons

2 eggs

1 cup milk

Flour, for dredging

Pinch of sea or kosher salt

Freshly ground black pepper

Corn or safflower oil, for frying

Split the frog leg pairs and remove the feet by cutting at the joints. Place the frog legs in a shallow baking dish and drizzle the lemon juice over them. Roll the legs in the lemon juice to coat evenly. Cover and refrigerate for at least 4 hours or overnight.

In a bowl, beat the eggs and milk with a whisk. Place the flour on a plate. Rinse the legs, pat dry, and season with salt and pepper. Roll the legs in the flour, shake off the excess, and then dip in the egg batter.

Heat a cast-iron skillet over medium-high heat. Place enough oil in the pan to lightly coat the bottom. Transfer 4 or 5 legs to the pan at a time to avoid overcrowding. Cook, turning once, for 5 to 6 minutes on each side, until golden brown and cooked through. Transfer to paper towels and keep warm until all the legs are cooked. Serve warm.

FROG LEGS WITH TOASTED PECANS: After cooking all of the frog legs, add $1/2$ cup toasted and chopped pecans, 2 tablespoons chopped green onion, juice of 1 lemon, and 2 tablespoons butter to the pan. Pour the sauce over the frog legs or pass separately.

CONCH FRITTERS COLOMBIAN-STYLE ||| Called *caracol* throughout

Latin America, some conchs are now protected due to overharvesting. Conch meat has a delicious flavor reminiscent of clams. Use clams or mussels in this recipe if conch is unavailable. Serve these fritters with Wild Ginger Dipping Sauce (page 36) or a hot chile sauce, as they would in Colombia. ||| SERVES 4

$^{1}/_{2}$ cup unbleached all-purpose flour

1 tablespoon baking powder

1 egg

1 teaspoon water

1 small red bell pepper, finely chopped

1 small hot chile, seeded and finely chopped

4 pitted black ripe olives, sliced

1 green onion, white part only, chopped

2 cloves garlic, finely chopped

1 pound conch meat, pounded and finely chopped

Corn oil, for frying

In a bowl, combine the flour and baking powder. Mix with a fork to blend. Whisk the egg with the water in a separate bowl. Make a well in the center of the flour mixture and pour the egg in the well. Using the fork, gently stir the flour into the egg, just to moisten. Do not overmix. Fold in the bell pepper, chile, olives, green onion, garlic, and conch meat just to combine.

Pour the oil to a depth of 1 inch into heavy sauté pan over medium-high heat. The oil must be quite hot, about 365°F. To test if the oil is ready to cook, drop a pea-sized piece of batter in the oil. If it browns nicely within a couple of minutes, the oil is ready. Spoon teaspoon-sized pieces of the batter into the oil, 3 or 4 at a time, being careful not to overcrowd the pan. Cook for 4 to 6 minutes, until the first side turns golden brown. With tongs, turn the fritters over and cook for 4 to 6 minutes, until the other side is golden brown. Using tongs, transfer to paper towels and keep warm until all of the fritters are cooked. Serve at once.

STURGEON WITH WILD MUSHROOMS AND LEEKS |||

Though sturgeon has now been relegated to dammed reservoirs and a few rivers, one can still angle for this ancient fish. The roe was prized by early peoples, as it is today, and the meat has an almost veal-like quality that makes preparation very simple. Smoked sturgeon was eaten by many tribes from the Atlantic to the Pacific and remains a global delicacy. Serve this dish with Cattail Cakes (page 165) or steamed cattail shoots. ||| SERVES 4

2 tablespoons sunflower seeds

8 (3-ounce) thin slices sturgeon

1/4 teaspoon sea or kosher salt

1/4 teaspoon freshly ground black pepper

Corn, potato, or arrowroot flour, for dredging

2 tablespoons sunflower, corn, or safflower oil

1/2 pound wild or cremini mushrooms, sliced

4 wild leeks, or 1 cultivated leek, white part only, sliced

2 sunchokes, cut into 1/4-inch slices

1 cup chicken white stock (page 209) or water

Preheat the oven to 350°F. Spread the sunflower seeds on a baking sheet and toast for 3 to 5 minutes, until golden brown.

Season the fish with salt and pepper and then dredge in the flour, shaking off any excess. Heat the oil in a heavy sauté pan over medium-high heat. Add the fish and cook, turning once, for about 3 minutes on each side, until browned and cooked through. Transfer to a warm platter and keep warm.

Place the mushrooms and leeks in the sauté pan over medium-high heat. Cook, stirring occasionally, for 3 to 5 minutes, until softened but not browned. Add the sunflower seeds and sunchokes and cook for 2 minutes. Increase the heat to high and add the stock. Cook for 7 to 10 minutes, until reduced by two-thirds. The sauce should still be liquid but slightly thickened. Adjust the seasoning with salt and pepper if necessary. Spoon the sauce over the fish or pass separately. Serve at once.

PHOTO BY MARSHALL H. SAVILLE

CHAPTER SEVEN

BREADS &
SAVORY CAKES

≋ Maya (?) women making bread, 1900. Palenque, Chiapas, Mexico. (N37556)

147

While flour from wheat grain is now widely used throughout the Western Hemisphere, the indigenous people of the Americas have long incorporated flours from other sources into their cuisine. Until the sixteenth century, acorn and mesquite flours were staples for the tribes of the southwestern United States. Flours derived from cattail and wapato were necessities for Great Plains and Plateau communities, and manioc, amaranth, and corn flour remain common ingredients for Central and South American peoples.

Originating in Central America nearly ten thousand years ago, corn, or maize, became an indispensable staple for most Native people, and it continues to play a central role in many American Indian beliefs and rituals. According to the Jakaltek Maya, the First Father distributed corn among the leaders of distant communities, spreading it across North America. In nearly every ceremony, Pueblo peoples of the arid Southwest pray for rain, corn, and renewal. For most Iroquois and southeastern tribes, the Green Corn Ceremony, which marks the emergence of a new crop, symbolizes not only the beginning of a new year but also a spiritual fresh start. On the North American Plains, where corn was grown by tribes that had settled in the fertile river valleys, it was dried and preserved in many different ways, then traded for buffalo products with more nomadic Plains people. While fry bread made with wheat flour has become among the best known of all Native foods, corn and the breads and cakes that evolved from it have a far more deeply rooted presence in most American Indian cultures.

FRY BREAD |||

This recipe for fry bread was developed from various recipes found throughout the United States. It was inspired by Clara Rose LaTray Nordberg (Turtle Mountain Band of Chippewa), Marlene's mother. Fry bread appears to have been produced in some form by all North American Native peoples after European contact. It has many wonderful uses, ranging from a splendid breakfast accompaniment to a foil for braised dishes. It is fabulous when filled with your favorite sandwich ingredients and is hard to beat as a midday snack when sprinkled liberally with cinnamon and sugar. For the best quality, fry bread must be served immediately after preparation. ||| MAKES 8 TO 12 SMALL BREADS OR 6 TO 8 LARGE BREADS

3 cups unbleached all-purpose flour, plus extra for dusting

1 tablespoon baking powder

1 teaspoon sea or kosher salt

1¼ cups warm water

Corn oil, for frying

In a bowl or on a clean working surface, combine the flour, baking powder, and salt. Make a well in the center of the flour and pour the warm water into the center of the well. Using a wooden spoon or your hands, work the flour into the water. Gently knead the dough into a ball and form it into a log about 3 inches in diameter. Cover the dough with a clean kitchen towel to prevent drying and let it relax for at least 10 minutes. The dough is best used within a few hours, although it may be used the next day if covered tightly with plastic wrap and refrigerated. Return to room temperature before using.

To form the bread, place the dough on a cutting board. Cut the log in half with a dough cutter or knife. Continue to cut each section in half to the desired thickness. Cut small pieces for appetizers and larger pieces for sandwiches. Cover the dough as you cut to prevent drying.

Lightly flour a work surface. Place some flour on a plate. Lightly dust each piece of dough with the flour and place on the work surface. With a rolling pin, roll each piece to about ¼ inch thick. Place each rolled piece in the flour on the plate, turning and lightly coating. Shake gently to remove excess flour. Stack the rolled pieces on a plate. Cover with a dry kitchen towel until ready to cook.

Pour the oil into a deep, wide saucepan to a depth of 1 inch. Place over medium-high heat. When the oil is hot, place 1 or 2 pieces of dough at a time in the pan. Do not overcrowd. Cook, turning once, for 2 to 3 minutes on each side. This bread generally does not brown and should be dry on the exterior and moist in the center. Try cooking one piece first, let it cool, and taste for doneness. This will give you a better gauge of how to proceed with

(CONTINUED)

the balance of the bread, ensuring good results. Remove the breads from the oil with tongs or a fork and place on paper towels to absorb excess oil. Serve immediately.

GRILL BREAD: Prepare a medium-hot fire in a charcoal grill or preheat a gas grill to medium-high. Prepare and cut the dough according to the recipe for fry bread. After rolling out the dough, place the pieces on the grill rack. Cook for 2 to 3 minutes, until bubbles form and the dough has risen slightly. Turn over and cook for 2 to 3 minutes, until the surface appears smooth and is dry to the touch. This bread cooks quickly and is best when moist in the center, with a pliant crust. Some browning occurs, but generally speaking, this is a blond bread. Serve immediately.

CORN TORTILLAS ||| Tortillas are among the first preparations made from cultivated plants

perfected by Mesoamerican cooks. The peoples of Central America were making these breads for thousands of years before the Conquest. Every day, Aztec people ate unleavened, round, flatbreads of many different sizes and thicknesses. The conquistadors used the Spanish word *tortilla* to describe them all. ||| Fresh masa and masa harina may be purchased at Latin American markets. The difference between the two is that fresh masa is ready to use and has a superior flavor. If using masa harina, look for flour produced in Mexico, Honduras, or Guatemala, and look for the term *nixta-malizado,* indicating the flour was processed from nixtamal. ||| To shape the tortillas, you'll need a metal or wooden tortilla press available at most Latin American markets. Line the press with a 2-quart plastic bag to reduce sticking. Cut the bag in half and use one piece for each side of the press. ||| MAKES 12 (6-INCH) TORTILLAS

2 cups fresh tortilla masa (nixtamal),
or masa harina from nixtamal

About 1 1/2 cups tepid water (used only
with masa harina)

TORTILLA TERMINOLOGY

Nixtamal is the name of the mixture after corn kernels have been dried and cooked briefly in unslaked lime and water. The process is called nixtamalization. The wet, fresh-ground nixtamal is called *masa* in Mexico; *masa harina* is a commercially produced flour made from the nixtamal. A *metate,* made from a porous lava stone, is shaped like a flat trough and is used to grind the nixtamal into masa. A *comal* is a ceramic griddle used to cook tortillas. *Chiquihuitl* or *tlaxcal* is an indigenous term for a special basket made to hold tortillas.

To prepare tortillas using fresh tortilla masa, proceed to the shaping step below.

To prepare tortillas using masa harina, first reconstitute the masa harina. Place the masa harina in a bowl. Make a well in the center of the flour and pour the water into the well. Using your hands, fold the flour into the water and work into a pliant ball. Masa harina varies in processing and age, and may require a bit more or less water. If the dough is too dry, the tortillas will crack on the tortilla press; if it is too wet, it will stick.

To shape the tortillas, divide the masa mixture and form into 12 balls. Cover with a clean kitchen towel to keep moist. One at a time, place the masa balls on the tortilla press, close the press, and apply even pressure. The thickness of the tortillas is regulated by the amount of pressure applied. Apply light pressure for a thick tortilla or more pressure for a thinner tortilla, depending on the intended use. Open the press and remove the tortilla.

To cook the tortillas, place a *comal* or dry cast-iron skillet over medium-high heat. Add a tortilla and cook for 2 to 3 minutes, until lightly browned and set. Turn and cook the second side for 2 to 3 minutes, until the tortillas are lightly colored and just cooked through. (Mesoamerican cooks turn the tortillas as often as necessary.) You may choose to place the cooked tortillas in a special napkin-lined basket called a *chiquihuitl* or *tlaxcal* until all of the tortillas have been cooked, or you may simply cover the tortillas with a clean cloth to keep them warm and moist.

Tortillas are exquisite when served freshly made, but are also quite acceptable when reheated. If you are planning to reheat the tortillas, cook them for 1 to 2 minutes on each side, until just set. Cover with a cloth and let cool to room temperature. To reheat, place the tortillas on the comal or in a dry cast-iron skillet over medium-high heat and cook for 1 1/2 to 2 minutes on each side, until warmed through. Reheated tortillas lack the steam created when the dough is freshly cooked. To assure moist, fresher-tasting tortillas, simply dip your fingers into water and sprinkle around, not on, the tortillas to create steam. Take care not to add too much water, which will result in a mushy tortilla.

Celebrating Corn

Pounding the pestle
against a white stone,
she grinds last year's kernels to meal.
> *I have planted my corn*

A thin white-gold powder
clings to her hands.
Around her, air shimmers.
> *I have planted it with my song*

One of the puppies is barking,
staccato *yap yap*
punctuating her strokes.
> *Let it grow tall and beautiful*

Beside her, an aunt stitches
shell beads to deerskin, as young women
lean toward clay pots, stirring embers.
> *washed in sunlight*

The men are out gathering
red clay for ocher. Beyond domed
bark houses, fields
> *watered by rains*

stretch small earthen mounds
toward the river. Redbuds blossom,
their branches upturned like hands.
> *Grandmother, we plant our seeds*

—Karenne Wood (Monacan)
(see page 176)

≈ Eastern Cherokee woman gathering corn, North Carolina, 1908. (N2736)

FRESH CORN DUMPLINGS |||

As the knowledge of corn cultivation spread from its source in central Mexico seven to ten thousand years ago, so too did a type of corn dumpling. Maya and Aztec tamales are a form of corn dumpling, and they typify a cake-like bread now made by such divergent cultures as the Oneida and the O'odham. ||| These are extremely light dumplings, without much of the unwanted cholesterol usually associated with this dish. Preparation couldn't be simpler. Try them soon after the corn in your area is ripe, and serve with Buffalo Chili (page 68). ||| MAKES ABOUT 16 DUMPLINGS; SERVES 4

2 cups fresh corn kernels (about 2 ears)

1 cup unbleached all-purpose flour

3 tablespoons cornmeal

2 teaspoons baking powder

1¼ teaspoons sea or kosher salt

¼ cup unsalted butter, at room temperature

1 to 2 tablespoons milk

2 cups brown, white, or vegetable stock (pages 208, 209, and 207)

Place the corn kernels in a bowl and mash with a fork. Alternatively, place the kernels in the bowl of a food processor and pulse until coarse and unevenly textured. Combine the flour, cornmeal, baking powder, and 1 teaspoon of the salt in a bowl and mix well. Add the corn and fold the ingredients together. Cut in the butter. Add enough milk to form a stiff batter.

Preheat the oven to 400°F. Place the stock and the remaining ¼ teaspoon salt in a large, lidded sauté pan over medium-high heat and bring to a simmer. Form walnut-sized portions of the batter into ovals, and drop them into the pan. Cover tightly and place in the oven for 10 to 12 minutes, until a knife tip or toothpick inserted into the center comes out clean. To ensure lightness, do not uncover the dumplings during cooking.

Remove from the oven, ladle into bowls, and serve at once.

≈ Kiva dough bowl, Santa Domingo Pueblo, circa 1850. New Mexico. (5/841)

CORNMEAL CAKES ||| These cakes, made by communities in the southeastern United States, are good with gravy or served with simple roasts, stews, or braised dishes. ||| MAKES 12 CAKES

3 cups chicken white stock (page 209)

2¼ cups milk

1 tablespoon sea or kosher salt

½ teaspoon freshly ground black pepper

3 cups white cornmeal or grits

6 tablespoons unsalted butter

1 tablespoon oil, for frying

Line a 5 by 7½-inch baking dish with plastic wrap.

Combine the stock, milk, salt, and pepper in a heavy saucepan and bring to a boil over medium-high heat. Gradually stir in the cornmeal and cook, stirring constantly, for 25 to 30 minutes, until the mixture is thick and pulls away from the sides of the pan. Stir in the butter until melted. Transfer to the prepared baking dish and spread out evenly to about 1¼ inches thick, being sure to fill in any voids. Place in the refrigerator and allow to cool completely.

Cut the cooled mixture into squares or triangles about 2½ inches in size. Heat the oil in a cast-iron skillet over medium heat. Add the cakes a few at a time and fry, turning once, for 5 to 7 minutes on each side, until golden brown. (For a lighter version, the cakes can be broiled. Lightly oil a baking sheet, lay the cakes on the sheet, and broil, turning once, for 4 to 6 minutes, until golden brown.) Serve at once.

CORNMEAL WAFFLES ||| Cornmeal used on its own in this recipe produces a dense cake that has broad use and appeal. However, when cornmeal is used in tandem with wheat flour and cooked in this Old World manner, a crisp and elegant waffle is produced. Try serving these for lunch with roast turkey and gravy, or with braised meat with plenty of the savory braising liquid. ||| MAKES 4 TO 5 WAFFLES

1¼ cups unbleached all-purpose flour

½ cup cornmeal

¼ cup masa harina or corn flour

1 teaspoon sea or kosher salt

4 teaspoons baking powder

3 tablespoons sugar

2 eggs

½ cup buttermilk

1 cup milk

⅔ cup corn oil

In a large bowl, combine the flour, cornmeal, masa, salt, baking powder, and sugar and mix well. In a separate large bowl, combine the eggs, buttermilk, milk, and corn oil and mix well. Add the dry ingredients to the wet ingredients and stir well to form a thick batter. Bake according to the manufacturer's instructions on a well-oiled waffle iron.

ACORN BREAD |||

Acorns have long been an important food for Native people in North America. Although there are many varieties of oak trees, few provide acorns that are acceptable for human consumption. The best-tasting acorns are those with the least amount of tannin. The Maidu and the Pomo people of California employ a traditional means of tannin extraction. Acorns are cracked, peeled, and ground in stone mortars. The nut meal is then encased in a mesh bag and held under running water until the milky liquid clears and the bitter taste is removed. Acorn meal is typically blended with cornmeal or wheat flour, as is done in this recipe. Traditionally, the Pomo would cook the bread on a fire-heated stone. ||| MAKES 1 LOAF

1 cup acorn meal

¹/₂ cup cornmeal

¹/₂ cup whole wheat flour

1 teaspoon coltsfoot ash or sea salt

1 tablespoon baking powder

1 egg

3 tablespoons walnut or hazelnut oil

¹/₄ cup honey

1 cup milk

Preheat the oven to 350°F. Oil and flour a 5 by 9-inch loaf pan (or use a nonstick pan).

In a bowl, combine the acorn meal, cornmeal, whole wheat flour, coltsfoot ash, and baking powder and mix well. In a separate bowl, whisk the egg until well blended. Add the oil, honey, and milk to the egg and whisk until blended thoroughly. Pour the egg mixture over the dry ingredients. Using a wooden spoon or rubber spatula, fold the liquid ingredients into the dry ingredients until just moistened. Do not overmix.

Pour the batter into the prepared loaf pan and bake for 20 to 25 minutes, until an toothpick inserted into the center of the loaf comes away clean. Remove from the oven and cool in the pan on a wire rack for about 5 minutes. Gently tap the corner of the pan to remove the bread. Place the bread on the rack to cool or serve warm.

≈ Cahuilla woman preparing acorns for grinding, Southern California. (P00501)

BUCKSKIN CAKES ||| Buckskin cakes were named for their color: when cooked over a steady, gentle heat on a hot stone or in a cast-iron skillet, the cake surface takes on a splendid golden-brown hue that resembles tanned hide. Before the introduction of wheat flour, these cakes were made from cattail flour in some locales. Improvise freely when preparing these delicious biscuit-like cakes, adding pine nuts, finely chopped pumpkin seeds, or other regional herbs and flavorings to the basic recipe. Plain, they are best with smoked salmon, or with some cured salmon roe and a spoonful of crema (page 209). The cakes also double as a sweet when served with nut butter and Raw Fresh Berry Jam (page 178), or try serving them with honey and butter for breakfast. ||| MAKES 6 (4-INCH) CAKES

$1/2$ cup pumpkin seeds, sunflower seeds, sesame seeds, or pine nuts, or a blend of your choosing

2 cups unbleached all-purpose flour

1 teaspoon coltsfoot ash or sea salt

2 teaspoons baking powder

$3/4$ to 1 cup water

2 tablespoons pumpkin, hazelnut, walnut, or sunflower oil

In batches if necessary, place the seeds in a spice mill, coffee grinder, or food mill and grind coarsely.

In a bowl, combine the ground seeds, flour, coltsfoot ash, and baking powder and mix well with a fork. Add enough water to form a soft, pliant ball of dough. Place in a bowl, cover with a dry kitchen towel, and leave to relax at room temperature for 2 to 3 hours.

Divide the dough into 6 equal pieces. Shape each piece into a cake 4 inches wide and $1/2$ inch thick. Heat the oil in a heavy sauté pan over medium-high heat. Add the cakes to the pan and fry, turning once, for 7 minutes on each side, until puffed and golden brown. Serve warm.

TOASTED FILBERT CAKES ||| Peoples of the Northeast harvested hazelnuts, acorns,

walnuts, hickory nuts, and other species throughout the fall. This modern recipe for hand-patted little cakes combines

Old and New World ingredients. Serve the cakes with a small, wilted salad of dandelion greens, roasted root vegetables,

or with fresh grilled apples and crema (page 209). ||| MAKES 4 CAKES

1 (10-inch) flour tortilla, or 6 plain
    wheat crackers

1 cup hazelnuts

$^1/_4$ teaspoon minced fresh basil

$^1/_2$ teaspoon minced fresh thyme

$^1/_4$ teaspoon minced fresh marjoram

1 ramp or green onion, white part only,
    minced

1 cup grated aged or medium cheese, such
    as manchego, Muenster, or Gruyère

$^1/_4$ teaspoon sea or kosher salt

$^1/_4$ teaspoon freshly ground black pepper

1 egg

Corn or nut oil, for cooking

Preheat the oven to 350°F. Place the tortilla in the oven and cook for 10 to 12 minutes, until dried and brittle. Remove from the oven and allow to cool. Maintain the oven temperature at 350°F. When cool enough to handle, break the tortilla into small pieces.

Spread the hazelnuts on a baking sheet. Place in the oven and cook, turning occasionally, for 12 to 15 minutes, until toasted. Remove from the oven and allow to cool. When cool enough to handle, place the nuts in a kitchen towel and rub vigorously to remove as much of the papery skins as possible.

Combine the tortilla, hazelnuts, basil, thyme, marjoram, ramp, cheese, salt, and pepper in a bowl and toss lightly. Transfer to a food processor and pulse to achieve a coarsely chopped, rough texture, or use a potato masher or pastry cutter and break the mixture into a coarse meal. In a separate bowl, beat the egg with a fork. Fold the egg into the nut mixture. Turn the dough out onto a floured work surface. Knead by hand for a few minutes to fully incorporate the ingredients.

To form the cakes, separate the dough into 4 pieces. Shape each piece into a round cake $^1/_2$ to $^3/_4$ inch thick and smooth the sides. To cook the cakes, heat a cast-iron skillet over medium heat and add some oil. Add the cakes and cook, turning once, for about 5 minutes on each side, until a toothpick or knife inserted into the center comes out clean. Serve immediately.

CORNMEAL CRACKERS ||| Substitute blue cornmeal or masa harina for the unbleached

flour for a truly authentic indigenous cracker. Acorn flour, cattail pollen, and cattail flour are terrific substitutes as well.

Try these crackers plain or sprinkled with your favorite toasted seed or fresh herb just prior to baking. ||| MAKES

ABOUT 100 CRACKERS

1¹/₂ cups unbleached all-purpose flour

¹/₂ cup cornmeal

¹/₄ teaspoon table salt

2 tablespoons unsalted butter

About 1 cup water

1 tablespoon sea or kosher salt

Preheat the oven to 325 °F.

In a bowl, combine the flour, cornmeal, and table salt and mix well with a fork. With the fork, cut the butter into the flour mixture until it resembles coarse meal. Bring the water to a boil and then remove from the heat. Allow to cool slightly. Adding it gradually, stir just enough of the water into the dough so that a ball forms.

Divide the dough into 4 equal pieces. One at a time, place each piece on a floured surface, pastry cloth, or between 2 pieces of plastic wrap and roll out to about ¹/₈ inch thick. Sprinkle with salt. With the tines of a fork, make impressions about 1 inch apart over the entire surface of the dough. Leave the sheets whole or cut into 2-inch squares (or another desired shape). With a metal spatula, gently transfer to an ungreased baking sheet. If you're cutting, you should get 25 crackers from each sheet of dough. Bake for 15 to 20 minutes, until lightly browned. Transfer to wire racks and allow to cool before serving. Break the whole sheets into the desired shape and size. These crackers will keep for up 7 days in a tightly covered container. To re-crisp, toast in a 400 °F oven for 3 to 4 minutes.

ACORN CRACKERS: Add ³/₄ cup acorn flour. Decrease the all-purpose flour to ³/₄ cup and the water to ³/₄ cup. Increase the butter to 3¹/₂ table-spoons.

CATTAIL CRACKERS: Add ³/₄ cup cattail flour or pollen. Decrease the all-purpose flour to ³/₄ cup. Replace the water with milk, and decrease the amount to ³/₄ cup. Increase the butter to 3 tablespoons.

≈ Walla Walla cornhusk leggings, late 1800s. (10/8091)

WILD MUSTARD SEED AND ALLIUM CRACKERS |||

Traditional wild onions, called *pshi-n* by the Dakota, *shi-n hop* by the Winnebago, and *osidiwa* by Pawnee elders are part of a genus (*Allium*) that also includes garlic, chives, leeks, and shallots. These portable flatbreads were made with other flours such as cattail and acorn before the introduction of wheat. Crackers are so easy to prepare it is a wonder more cooks don't make them at home. Break the large, irregular sheets to suit your needs or cut them into shapes before baking. ||| MAKES 65 TO 70 CRACKERS

2 tablespoons wild or cultivated mustard seed

2 cups unbleached all-purpose flour

1¹/₂ teaspoons sea or kosher salt

1 teaspoon freshly ground black pepper

¹/₂ cup unsalted butter

1 cup minced wild onion or green onions, white and green parts

1 to 2 tablespoons water

Preheat the oven to 375°F.

Place the mustard seeds in a spice mill, food mill, or coffee grinder and grind to a very fine powder. In a bowl, combine the mustard powder, flour, salt, and pepper and mix well. Cut the butter into the dry ingredients until the mixture resembles coarse meal. Add the onion and enough water to form a firm ball.

Divide the dough into 2 pieces and roll each out to ¹/₈ inch thick. With the tines of a fork, make impressions about 1 inch apart over the entire surface of the dough. Leave the sheets whole or cut into 2-inch squares (or another desired shape). With a metal spatula, gently transfer to an ungreased baking sheet. If you're cutting, you should get about 30 crackers from each sheet of dough. Bake for 20 to 25 minutes, until browned and dry. Transfer to wire racks and allow to cool before serving. Break the whole sheets into the desired shape and size. These crackers will keep for up to 7 days in a tightly covered container. To re-crisp, toast in a 400°F oven for 3 to 4 minutes.

Foraging for Cattails

OUR FAMILY WENT to the central Oregon coast to forage for traditional indigenous foods of the coastal peoples. Veteran guide Lee Gray was our host. Lee has devoted his life to the study of Native foods and low-impact foraging.

Our foray began at an inland stand of cattails. We donned our knee-high rubber boots for good reason. Cattails occur in thick mud that nearly bested us. While our son, Zoey, gathered the tender new cobs, Marlene's job was to harvest cattail pollen. To harvest the bright-yellow pollen, she would take the cattail stalk, tip it into her container and gently shake. Off came the pollen!

It is a different world, standing in the middle of a thick forest of cattails. Marlene could hear the voices of her fellow gatherers, but she couldn't see anyone. "As I was harvesting, my thoughts wandered back to my own ancestors. My great-great-great-great-grandmother was named Sinks in the Earth. So there I was, harvesting cattail pollen and sinking into the earth. 'I'm sinking! I'm stuck!' I was laughing and fondly thinking, 'Sinks in the Earth, look at your granddaughter!'"

—Fernando and Marlene Divina

≈ Large Hupa seed-gathering basket, circa 1900. To collect seeds, women bent grass stems over the mouths of close-twined, conical baskets like this one and beat the grass with a wicker beater or a stick. The seeds were parched over hot coals before being stored or ground. (8/2943)

CATTAIL CAKES ||| Cattails were a staple commodity for many early cultures, used to make not

only bedding and clothing but also delicious foods. The Zapotec of Oaxaca at one time revered the plant so highly that they made a shrine, called El Tule, in the form of a stand of cattails with a massive tree at its center. Today, the tree alone survives as a tourist attraction, long after the usefulness of the *tules*, or cattails, waned. ||| Native peoples continue to use cattails as a source for weaving materials and, occasionally, for food. In the fall, roots provide a starchy tuber that can be stored for winter use or eaten fresh. The roots can be baked, boiled, or ground into flour for use in breads. Spring yields tender shoots that can be eaten as a salad or as a pot vegetable in stews. It is possible to cook and eat the cob-like spikes just as one eats corn. In summer, the pollen can be harvested and combined with the root flour, or with other flours, to make tasty and nutritious savory cakes and breads. Cattail pollen, high in niacin, has a texture similar to finely milled flour, and it lends a slight floral flavor. Cattail products are available via mail order (see sources, page 215). ||| Serve these unusual cakes with roast duckling and a sauce made of the natural roasting juices, or serve them as an accompaniment to a roast chicken or turkey with gravy. They are also excellent when served warm with honey or Raw Fresh Berry Jam (page 178) for breakfast. ||| MAKES 6 (3-INCH) CAKES

1 cup cattail flour or cattail pollen

1 cup unbleached all-purpose flour

1 tablespoon plus 1 teaspoon baking powder

1 teaspoon coltsfoot ash or sea salt

1 to 1½ cups warm water

1 teaspoon hazelnut or corn oil

In a bowl, combine the cattail flour, all-purpose flour, baking powder, and coltsfoot ash and mix well with a fork to blend thoroughly. With your hands, mix in enough of the water to form a soft, pliant dough. The dough should hold its shape but not feel tacky.

Divide the dough into 6 equal pieces. Shape each piece into a cake 3 inches wide and ¾ inches thick. You could also cut out the cakes with a biscuit cutter. Heat a heavy sauté pan over medium-low heat. Pour the oil into the pan, and, using a paper towel, spread the oil over the entire surface of the bottom of the pan to coat lightly and evenly. Place the cakes in the pan and cook, turning once, for 5 to 7 minutes on each side, until the surface is golden brown.

Serve at once or store in a paper bag at room temperature and reheat before serving. To reheat, wrap the cakes in aluminum foil and place on the center rack of a 350°F oven for 5 to 10 minutes, or heat them, uncovered, in a microwave for 15 seconds on medium.

CHAPTER EIGHT

SWEETS & DESSERTS

≈ *Food Trading,* Arlo Nouvayouma (Hopi). (S23/7450)

Of all the cross-cultural preparations that we now enjoy, desserts have benefited the most from diversity. New World flavorings such as chocolate, vanilla, maple sugar, and berries have combined well with milk, wheat flour, refined sugar, and domesticated eggs from the Old World to produce delicious concoctions. Before contact with Europeans, Native cooks enhanced the natural sugars in berries by mashing and boiling the fruit with maple syrup or honey, by drying it, or by using a combination of the two methods to produce portable, long-lasting cakes that could later be reconstituted. In the Northwest Coast, a feast dish was made of mixed dried berries beaten with eulachon (candlefish) oil and snow. In the Southwest, wildflowers, cactus fruit, and the sugar in corn provided sources of sweetness for bread and cake batter.

Most people would agree that the world's favorite sweet food—"the food of the gods," as the famed botanist Linnaeus called it—is chocolate. The cacao tree, native to Central and South America, provides the raw material for chocolate. Both the Maya and Aztec people prized cacao, using the beans not only for culinary purposes but also for trade and as money. Pre-Conquest chocolate was almost always a drink, which had many forms and flavorings (chile powders were among the most popular). Pounded maize could be added, but the highest aristocrats almost always took chocolate unadulterated, with a froth created by pouring the liquid from vessel to vessel. Chocolate also was of major ceremonial importance to the Maya and the Aztecs. It was served at lavish banquets, buried with the dead, and used to anoint newborn babies.

Pumpkin Fry Bread |||

This bread can be made with sweet potatoes, persimmons, and acorn squash—all indigenous foods of the Americas—and also with ripe plantains, with delicious results. Just replace the pumpkin with an equal amount of any of these ingredients. This dough is best when worked only enough to form and cook. Excess handling develops gluten, making the bread tough and dry. To serve, try dusting the fry bread with sugar flavored with cinnamon and a little ground nutmeg, clove, and allspice, or serve with a scoop of Honey Ice Cream (page 182). Mesquite flour can be purchased via mail order (see sources, page 214). ||| MAKES 12 BREADS

3 cups unbleached all-purpose flour,
    plus extra for dusting

1 cup mesquite flour, or 1/2 cup
    whole wheat flour

1/2 teaspoon sea or kosher salt

2 1/2 teaspoons baking powder

1/4 teaspoon ground cinnamon

1 cup pumpkin purée

1/3 cup honey

3/4 cup warm water

1/2 tablespoon hazelnut oil

Corn oil, for frying

In a large bowl, combine the flours, salt, baking powder, and cinnamon and mix well. In a separate bowl, combine the pumpkin, honey, warm water, and nut oil. Make a well in the center of the flour and add the pumpkin mixture. Work the wet ingredients into the dry ingredients and form the dough into a smooth ball. Spread a thin layer of oil over the dough and cover with plastic wrap. Let rest for 10 minutes before rolling and shaping.

Lightly flour a work surface. Lightly flour your hands and break the dough into 12 pieces. Form the pieces into balls. Sprinkle flour over the balls and roll out to 1/4-inch-thick rounds. The dough may be slightly tacky, so sprinkle with flour as necessary to ease handling.

Pour oil into a heavy sauté pan to a depth of 1 inch. Place over medium-high heat. Place the breads in the pan, 1 or 2 at a time, and fry, turning once, for about 3 minutes on each side, until the dough puffs and turns golden brown. Using tongs, remove from the pan and place on paper towels to drain. Serve warm.

PANAMANIAN-STYLE FRY BREAD ||| Called *hojaldres* in Panama, this bread is

very similar to North American fry bread. Try dusting it with confectioners' sugar and cinnamon for a delicious treat.

||| MAKES 6 TO 8 BREADS

2³/₄ cups unbleached all-purpose flour

1¹/₂ teaspoons baking powder

1 teaspoon sugar

2 teaspoon sea or kosher salt

²/₃ cup milk

¹/₄ cup corn oil

Corn, peanut, or sunflower oil, for frying

In a bowl, combine the flour, baking powder, sugar, and salt and mix well. Make a well in the center of the flour and add the milk and ¹/₄ cup oil. Using your hands, work the flour into the milk and oil and knead softly for a few minutes to form a smooth, elastic dough. Cover the dough with plastic wrap and let stand at room temperature for at least 1 hour.

Lightly flour your hands. Divide the dough into 6 to 8 pieces and work each piece into a round disk about 4 inches by ¹/₄ inch thick.

Pour oil into a heavy sauté pan to a depth of 2 inches. Place over medium-high heat. One at a time, place the bread in the oil and cook, turning once, for about 3 minutes on each side, until golden brown. Using tongs, remove from the oil and transfer the bread to paper towels to drain. Serve warm.

WILD GRAPE DUMPLINGS ||| Grape dumplings are a favorite among the Choctaw

and Cherokee. Modern cooks may use fresh cultivated Concord grapes and juice to replace the wild grapes that were

traditionally used, although wild grapes can still be found in parts of the southeastern United States. Serve these

dumplings warm with a scoop of ice cream or whipped cream. ||| SERVES 4

DUMPLINGS

1 cup unbleached all-purpose flour

2 teaspoons baking powder

1 1/2 teaspoons sugar

1/4 teaspoon sea or kosher salt

2 tablespoons plus 1 3/4 teaspoons
   unsalted butter

1/4 cup plus 2 tablespoons milk

2 cups grape juice

2 cups wild or Concord grapes, seeded

About 1/3 cup sugar

To prepare the dumplings, combine the flour, baking powder, sugar, and salt in a bowl and mix well with a fork. Cut the butter into the flour mixture with the tines of the fork to resemble coarse meal. Stir the milk into the dough. Using your hands, form the dough into a smooth ball.

Lightly flour a work surface and pat the dough into a disk. Sprinkle the dough with a thin coat of flour. Lightly flour a rolling pin and roll out the dough to a thickness of about 1/4 inch. Cut the dough into 8 (2-inch) squares, using all of the dough.

To cook the dumplings, combine the grape juice, grapes, and sugar in a shallow, wide, heavy pot with a tight-fitting lid. Bring to a boil over high heat, and then decrease the heat to medium and simmer gently. Taste and add more sugar if the juice is too tart; add a bit of water if it is too sweet. Place the dumplings in the juice, cooking them in batches, if necessary, to avoid overcrowding. Cover the pan tightly, decrease the heat to medium-low, and simmer for 10 to 12 minutes, until the dumplings are plumped and cooked through. Divide the dumplings and juice among individual bowls and serve at once.

Baked Pumpkin with Corn and Apple Pudding

||| This festive autumn dessert was a perennial favorite among the people of the southwestern United States long before pies and leavened breads were introduced to the New World. This recipe was adapted from a version in E. Barrie Kavasch's *Enduring Harvests*. When available, small pumpkins make attractive individual serving dishes. Serve with a scoop of ice cream or whipped cream. ||| SERVES 4 TO 6

½ cup cornmeal

¾ cup pine nuts

4 (4-inch) pumpkins, or 1 (8-inch) pumpkin

3 tart green apples, coarsely chopped

½ cup apple cider or apple juice

½ cup milk

1 cup mixed dried fruits, such as apricots, peaches, wild plums, cherries, and cranberries

½ cup pure maple syrup or honey

¼ teaspoon ground mace

¼ teaspoon ground allspice

½ teaspoon ground cinnamon

Preheat the oven to 450°F. Spread the cornmeal on a baking sheet and place in the oven for 8 to 10 minutes to dry. Remove from the oven and decrease the heat to 350°F.

Spread the pine nuts on a baking sheet and place in the oven for 10 to 12 minutes, until toasted. Maintain the oven temperature at 350°F.

Cut around the pumpkin stems, leaving an inch of pumpkin around the stems, and remove the tops. Scrape out the seeds and reserve for another use. Set the pumpkins in a baking dish. If you are using a single large pumpkin, prick the flesh with a fork to facilitate even cooking.

Place the apples, cider, and milk in a saucepan over high heat. Bring to a boil, and then decrease the heat to medium. Simmer gently for about 10 minutes, until the apples are very tender. Pass through a fine-mesh sieve and return the liquid to the saucepan. Place the apples in a blender and process until smooth (or pass them through a food mill fitted with a medium-sized plate).

Return the apple purée to the saucepan over medium-high heat. Add the cornmeal, dried fruit, syrup, mace, allspice, and cinnamon and mix with a wooden spoon. Bring to a simmer and cook, stirring often, for 5 to 7 minutes. Add the pine nuts and mix well.

Distribute the pudding evenly among the pumpkins and replace the pumpkin tops. Place the baking dish in the oven and add about an inch of water to the dish. Bake for 35 to 40 minutes for individual pumpkins, 45 to 55 minutes for the large pumpkin, until the pumpkin is fork-tender. The pudding may tremble when removed from the oven, but should set to a creamy consistency when cooled slightly before serving. Serve warm.

BAKED PUMPKIN WITH CORN AND PEAR PUDDING: Replace the apples and apple cider with pears and pear cider.

CORNMEAL LOAF CAKE ||| This recipe adds dried fruit and nuts to a fried cornmeal cake that is made throughout the Northeast and Great Lakes regions. In their simplest form, fried or baked cornmeal cakes were known to Chippewa and Cree people as bannock (also the name of several other, very different breads). Marion Cunningham prepares a version in *The Breakfast Book*. The cake is delicious served with blackberry and apple purées and crema (page 209). Also, it is lovely as a dessert when warmed and served with fresh berries and a scoop of Honey Ice Cream (page 182). ||| MAKES 2 LOAVES

2 cups cornmeal

2 cups water

2 cups apple cider

1 cup pure maple syrup

1 teaspoon sea or kosher salt

1 cup plus 2 tablespoons unsalted butter

2 cups coarsely chopped hazelnuts or
    walnuts

2 cups dried fruits, such as wild grapes,
    wild plums, apricots, and cranberries

1/2 cup corn oil, for cooking

Line 2 (5 by 9-inch) loaf pans with plastic wrap.

Combine the cornmeal and water in bowl and mix well. Set aside to rest.

Place the cider, syrup, salt, and butter in a heavy saucepan over high heat. Bring to a boil. Add the cornmeal and water and decrease the heat to medium. Cook, stirring constantly, for 5 minutes, until the mixture comes away from the sides of the pan. Remove from the heat and fold in the nuts and dried fruits. Spread the batter into the prepared loaf pans. Allow to cool completely at room temperature, then cover and refrigerate for at least 2 hours or overnight.

Unmold the loaves onto a clean surface and slice into 1-inch pieces. Heat a cast-iron skillet over medium heat. Pour about 1 tablespoon of the oil into the pan. Place a few slices of cake in the pan and cook, turning once, for 3 to 5 minutes on each side, until browned. Repeat with the remaining slices, freshly oiling the pan for each batch. Transfer the cooked slices to a serving platter and keep warm until ready to serve.

Making Apple Butter

IN LATE SEPTEMBER, evenings bring Monacan women to the tribal center kitchen, where they make apple butter. They gather their aprons, headscarves tied on, descending the hillsides with dusk. The first night, they pare, core, and quarter cooking apples, imperfect yellow spheres stacked in bushel baskets—no crimson, waxed Delicious, no green Granny Smiths, no Empires. All evening, women chop as apple chunks turn the color of earth in the air, as leaves begin to yellow in the darkness. They need one quart of apples for every half pint; baskets empty as fingers grow moist, then wrinkle, among laughter and the scrapes of small knives that pare and pare again.

The second night, boiling begins. Scents of hot cider, cinnamon, ginger, and cloves rise to spread around the women like thick, hooded robes. Quarts of cider or vinegar are stirred and stirred again, the hours it takes to reduce each pot by half, to add the chopped apples, simmer an hour, add sugar, spices, boil again, until dark-gold mixtures turn the mahogany velvet of trees and the scent anoints the hair. Now, through the music of spoons, jars, and pots, through laughter, what remains is reduced to the essence of apple: roots and limbs laden with gold circles. We are blessed by the hands of these women who ladle into jars an enchantment made by heart, who condense, seal, process, and sell apple butter at St. Paul's church bazaar, three dollars for a pint.

—Karenne Wood

Karenne Wood (Monacan) has been honored as a Writer of the Year by the Wordcraft Circle of Native Writers and Storytellers. Her collection *Markings on Earth* won the Diane Decorah Award for Poetry from the Native Writers' Circle of the Americas. Wood, who serves on the Tribal Council of the Monacan Nation of Virginia, has worked as an environmentalist, an advocate for assistance to victims of domestic violence, and an activist for the rights of women and American Indians. She lives in Arlington, Virginia, with her family.

CHOCOLATE CRINKLE COOKIES

||| While chocolate wafers were part of every Aztec warrior's rations, the wafers had to be dissolved in water to make the drink that helped sustain the state's formidable armies. Chocolate in solid form was not introduced until the nineteenth century, but perhaps Moctezuma would have considered these now-popular cookies worthy of his own table. ||| MAKES ABOUT 36 COOKIES

1/3 cup unsalted butter

11 ounces bittersweet chocolate

1 cup sugar

1 1/2 tablespoons pure vanilla extract

2 1/3 cups unbleached all-purpose flour

1/4 cup unsweetened cocoa powder

1/4 teaspoon sea or kosher salt

1 teaspoon baking powder

5 eggs

2 cups confectioners' sugar

Place the butter, chocolate, and sugar in a large metal or ceramic bowl and place the bowl over a saucepan filled with water, or use a double boiler. Place the saucepan over medium-low heat. Stir constantly for about 10 minutes, until melted and smooth. Remove from the heat. Add the vanilla and stir until well blended.

In a separate bowl, combine the flour, cocoa, salt, and baking powder and mix well with a fork. Add the dry ingredients to the chocolate mixture and fold in with a rubber spatula. One at a time, add the eggs to the chocolate batter, beating with the spatula to fully incorporate each egg before adding the next. Cover and refrigerate for about 30 minutes, until the dough is firm to the touch.

Preheat the oven to 325°F. Lightly oil and flour 2 baking sheets (or use nonstick baking sheets).

Spread the confectioners' sugar on a plate. With a teaspoon, scoop out 1-inch pieces of the dough and drop them into the sugar. Roll to completely coat the dough. Arrange the cookies on the prepared baking sheets, spacing them about 3 inches apart. Try not to handle the cookies too much or the sugar will melt.

Place the cookies in the oven and bake for about 8 minutes, until they are cracked but still moist inside. If a few crumbs cling to an inserted toothpick, the cookies are still moist inside. Remove the cookies from the oven and let them cool on the baking sheets for about 5 minutes. Transfer to a wire rack and allow to cool completely before eating.

Raw Fresh Berry Jam ||| The flavor and texture of this wonderfully simple jam is based entirely on the ripeness of the fruit. Use thoroughly ripe fruit that yields easily under pressure and tastes sweet. As a general rule for determining ripeness, Ojibwe cooks suggest using only fruit that is easily removed or falls from the stem. ||| If you lack a mortar and pestle, use the tines of a fork or a potato masher. More sugar—even as much as twice the amount called for—may be needed if using naturally tart berries, such as salmonberries, gooseberries, or cranberries. Less sugar may be needed for very ripe raspberries, strawberries, blackberries, and blueberries. ||| MAKES ABOUT 1 CUP

1 cup ripe raspberries, strawberries, blackberries, blueberries, cranberries, salmonberries, or gooseberries

About 2 tablespoons sugar

1/2 to 3/4 teaspoon freshly squeezed lemon juice, strained

Place the berries in a mortar and pestle and process until coarsely mashed. (If using a blender or food processor, pulse to form a coarse consistency; do not overmix.) Add the sugar and lemon juice and mix well. Taste for balance and add additional sugar or lemon juice if necessary. Transfer the jam to a glass jar with a tight-fitting lid. Store in the refrigerator for 2 to 3 days or in the freezer for 2 to 3 months.

Cane Berry Preserve ||| Use this recipe for all types of cane berries (berries that grow on long prickly stems) including blackberries, raspberries, and salmonberries. In Alaska, red and pink nagoon berries are especially prized because, although sparse, they are easy to pick. ||| MAKES ABOUT 5 CUPS

6 cups blackberries, raspberries, or salmonberries

1/2 cup water

6 cups sugar

1 cup freshly squeezed orange juice

1/4 cup freshly squeezed lemon juice

1 tablespoon grated orange zest

Place the berries and water in a saucepan over high heat and bring to a boil. Add the sugar, orange juice, lemon juice, and zest and stir well. Bring to a full boil and then decrease the heat to medium. Simmer, stirring frequently, for 15 to 20 minutes, until the preserve reaches the jell stage.

To determine whether the preserve has reached the jell stage, spread 1 teaspoon into a thin layer on a plate. Place the plate in the coolest part of the refrigerator for 7 to 10 minutes, until completely chilled. Run your finger through the chilled preserve. If it separates and is not runny, the preserve is jelled. If it runs back together, continue cooking and test again.

When the preserve is jelled, remove from the heat and allow to cool completely. Transfer to a jar with a tight-fitting lid. Store in the refrigerator for up to 1 week.

FRESH BERRY LEATHER ||| Dried fruit leathers can be made from virtually any fruit and are excellent sources of nutrition and natural energy. This method of food preservation is a terrific alternative for putting up berries or fruits at the peak of their season. ||| MAKES ABOUT 12 PIECES

1 tablespoon corn oil

2 cups fresh blackberries, raspberries, or salmonberries

¹⁄₄ cup honey

Place the oven on the absolute lowest setting. Pour the oil onto a baking sheet and spread with a paper towel to thinly coat the entire surface.

Place the berries in a colander and fill a bowl with fresh water. Submerge the berries in the water bath and drain thoroughly, shaking gently to remove excess water. Place the berries and honey in a saucepan over high heat. Bring to a boil and then immediately remove from the heat. Transfer the berries to a blender and process until smooth.

Pour the purée onto the prepared baking sheet. Gently lift and tap the pan to evenly distribute the fruit mixture. Moisten a palette knife or rubber spatula. Shake off excess moisture and spread the fruit mixture as thinly as possible, leaving a solid, continuous sheet without streaking. (Or you can lift the pan a few inches off the counter and gently drop it to spread the purée.) Place the pan in the oven and cook for 4 to 8 hours, until completely dried. The fruit should be dry to the touch and slightly pliant and not brittle.

Remove from the oven and allow to cool completely. Using a pizza cutter, dough-cutting wheel, or knife, cut the leather into strips. Place the strips on plastic wrap and cover with another piece of wrap. Coil the strips and store in the refrigerator (or in a tight-fitting container at room temperature). The leather will keep for 2 to 3 weeks.

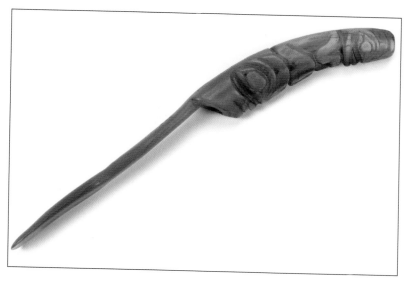

≈ Haida soapberry spoon carved with the likeness of the Dogfish (shark) and a human face. This flat spoon was used to eat berries that had been whipped into a froth. (20/2828)

BERRIES OF ABUNDANCE

BERRIES ARE AMONG THE ORIGINAL FOODS of the first people of the Western Hemisphere and can be found in all climatic zones. *Fragaria chiloensis,* a precursor to the modern strawberry and a coastal berry that was of particular interest to Thomas Jefferson, is one of the few species indigenous to both North and South America. It once grew along the Pacific coast from Alaska to Patagonia. This plant produced enormous firm fruit with brownish-red berries and ivory flesh. The leaves were thick, leathery, and shiny, obviously adapted to beach conditions. *Fragaria virginiana,* a wild strawberry indigenous to North America, was hybridized with *F. chiloensis* and became the base stock for modern strawberry varieties. Wild strawberries are usually best eaten uncooked, unlike other berries with less moisture.

Blueberries, one of the oldest foods the world over, can be found in numerous varieties throughout the Americas. Low-bush cranberries are in the same genus—*Vaccinium.* The classic cranberry sauce is made from these marshland berries.

Wild berries picked in season can translate to delicious pies, cobblers, jams, and fruit leathers to brighten dark winter days. In picking wild berries, there are a few caveats: don't pick or eat berries you have not positively identified. There are many reliable field guides available, and one should always be used. When in the forest, be on the lookout for other berry-lovers—especially bears! To free your hands for picking, attach a finely woven basket to your waist or fashion a bucket by cutting off the top of a plastic milk jug, leaving the handle to loop a belt through.

Blackberries are probably the easiest berry to find, as they grow nearly everywhere throughout both continents. There are several species of blackberries, a favorite being the trailing wild blackberry, *Rubus ursinus.* This berry is about 1/2 inch in diameter. The vines have a lot of thorns, so wear long sleeves and pants.

Another delicious wild berry to forage is the huckleberry. These berries can be found in areas that have been disturbed either by nature or by humans—burned or logged areas of forests are their preferred location. Varieties of these berries range in color from bright red to powder blue, black-blue, and purple. This pea-sized berry belongs to the *Vaccinium,* or blueberry, genus. It is much smaller than the blackberry, to which it is related.

The thimbleberry, *Rubus parviflorus,* is a member of the rose family. The most wonderful thing about thimbleberries, aside from their exquisite taste, is that the bush has no thorns, making them easy to pick. Thimbleberry bushes, which can often be found growing alongside trailing wild blackberries, are 4 to 5 feet high, on average. The berry looks like a powdered red raspberry and is quite delicate. You will need to use a gentle touch to pick this berry, and plan to enjoy it as trail food, as it simply will not hold up in a container for later use.

In Oregon, Washington, coastal Alaska, and British Columbia, salmonberries ripen as early as April. Wild strawberries may be ripe at the end of May. You'll find blackberries and huckleberries in the late summer and fall.

≈ Ojibwe bandolier bag, circa 1890.
Beaded cloth with a flower and berry motif. (23/9923)

HONEY ICE CREAM ||| From wildflower to maple blossom to mesquite—the subtle to strong tastes of various regional honeys provide a simple way to bring unique local flavor to the table. Serve this ice cream on Pumpkin Fry Bread (page 170), on warm Cornmeal Loaf Cake (page 175), or with chocolate sauce. |||

SERVES 4 TO 6

5 egg yolks

2 cups heavy cream

2 cups milk

3/4 cup honey

Place the egg yolks in a metal or ceramic bowl and whisk in the cream, milk, and honey. Transfer to a double boiler or a saucepan set over a larger pan of water and place over medium heat. Cook, stirring constantly with a wooden spoon, for 15 to 20 minutes, until the mixture is thick and creamy and there is no raw egg flavor. Remove from the heat and allow to cool completely.

Transfer to an ice cream maker and freeze according to the manufacturer's instructions. Serve immediately or cover tightly and store in the freezer for up to 2 days.

HUCKLEBERRY SORBET ||| Growing throughout the Western Hemisphere, these small red or blue berries have long provided people of the Americas with a delicious, accessible snack food. Picked by hand or shaken or gently brushed off the bush with a wooden rake, the fruit can be cleaned and separated from leaves and twigs by rolling it down a moistened board. Versatile and easy to preserve, dried huckleberries were a mainstay of the traditional winter diet for Northwest Coast people. The subtle flavors of different huckleberry varieties range from tart to deeply sweet, making this sorbet a truly regional dessert. Any wild berry will work for this recipe, although the amount of sugar and lemon juice needed may vary, depending on the tartness and ripeness of the berries. ||| MAKES ABOUT 2 CUPS

1 pound huckleberries

1 cup sugar

1 cup water

1/4 cup freshly squeezed lemon juice

Combine all of the ingredients in a saucepan over high heat. Mix well and bring to a boil. Boil hard for about 4 minutes, until the sugar is completely dissolved. Remove from the heat and allow to cool slightly. Transfer to a blender and process until smooth. Allow to cool completely.

Transfer to an ice cream maker and freeze according to the manufacturer's instructions. The sorbet is best served within a couple hours of preparation, but will keep for 3 to 4 days if tightly covered in the freezer.

HAUPIA ||| Haupia is a traditional luau food and was prepared in ti leaves in an imu fire pit. Chilling this custard-style dessert in toasted banana leaves gives it a fresh, tropical flavor, but it is delicious whether or not the leaves are used. ||| The coconut tree has long been called the most useful tree in the world, as practically every part of it can be utilized. Not only a food source, it is also used for textiles, baskets, and medicines. Coconut meat and milk are rich sources of complete protein and carbohydrates. Their only downside is a high concentration of saturated fat, particularly in the oil. *Pia* is the Hawaiian term for arrowroot, although it is also used to describe a type of yam starch.

||| SERVES 4 TO 6

2 banana leaves (optional)

2¹/₂ cups unsweetened coconut milk

³/₄ cup sugar

³/₄ cup water

¹/₂ cup pia (arrowroot) or cornstarch

Prepare a hot fire in a charcoal grill or preheat a gas grill to high. Lay the banana leaves on the grill rack for 2 to 3 minutes, until they turn brilliant green. Lay the leaves in a 1-quart baking dish, leaving enough length to overlap. If not using the banana leaves, lightly coat a 1-quart baking dish with vegetable or palm oil.

Combine the coconut milk, sugar, water, and pia in a saucepan over medium-high heat and stir well. Bring to a boil, stirring constantly, and then immediately remove from the heat. Pour into the prepared pan. Fold the leaves over to cover the mixture completely. Cover with plastic wrap and place in the refrigerator for at least 4 hours or overnight. The haupia should have the consistency of firm custard or soft cheese.

Open the banana leaves (or uncover the pan) and cut the haupia into squares or triangles to serve.

Molasses from a Tree

MY MOTHER REMEMBERS the way her uncle tapped maple trees back home at Kitigan Zibi, in Quebec. "We call the syrup *minotogonaminos,* which means 'molasses from a tree,'" she says. As a little girl, my mother, Mary Ann Miller, went to Uncle John's house with her parents, Clara and Camille Decontie, to help make the syrup in April. John Decontie lived near

PHOTO © 2003 BY MILLIE KNAPP

≈ Part of the maple syrup tree operation of the Kitigan Zibi Anishinabe Band Council, in Quebec.

Kitigan Zibi, or Garden River, where the maple trees grew. He notched about twenty trees with an ax and hung a galvanized bucket from each trunk to catch the sap, or sweet water, as she calls it. The whole process took about a week.

"I loved to drink the sweet water," she says about the clear, maple-flavored liquid that her mom or dad gave her in a cup dipped from one of the buckets. She was about six or seven when she watched Uncle John stir a big pot filled with sap over an open fire. Her parents helped with the stirring or gathered wood to keep the fire hot enough to boil the sap. They stirred and waited until it thickened, turned darker, and even began to taste like smoke. When it was ready, they poured it into leftover vinegar bottles for Uncle John to give away to neighbors and relatives, or to keep for his own family of eight children.

"We'd make pancakes and French toast with syrup. We'd eat it with bread, too," she says about those days more than sixty years ago. She recalls how her grandmother, Philomen Chabot, or Kokomis, as she called her, described how she used to boil the sap until it was fudge-like. Everyone ate it as candy or used it as sweetener for tea or coffee. Kokomis also told her that she used to pound raw blueberries and blend them with the fudge-like mix to make jam. "She told me that this is how they did it about a hundred years ago. They loved eating it when they had a sweet tooth back then," says my mom.

Today the Kitigan Zibi Band Council has developed a small maple syrup industry. Allen Cayer oversees the brewing at Awazibi Pure Maple Syrup, an oil-fired sap-processing plant that produces about 75 barrels of maple syrup each season. Before tapping, Cayer, Mike

Meness, and Gilbert Commanda set out on snowshoes atop 35 inches of snow in February. They check 11,700 taps and make necessary repairs within eight miles of tubing covering 150 acres of maple trees growing on a gentle mountain slope. They work numerous hours for the three weeks in April when the sap is flowing to maintain the tubing, the vacuum pumps, and the reverse osmosis machine, which processes the raw sap by eliminating up to 75 percent of the water to save on evaporation time. Cayer estimates that on average raw sap is 98 percent minerals and water and 2 percent sugar. *Awazibi* means "carrying water" in the Anishinabe language.

The idea for the commercial production came about six years ago when Chief Jean-Guy Whiteduck and the Band Council thought of using the forest in other ways than logging. Tom Ferguson wrote a business plan for the idea. "Quebec produces a large volume of the world's syrup," says Cayer.

Each season, the community is invited out to the sugar bush where the Awazibi plant is located. "We have ceremonies to thank the Creator for the harvest that we had," says Peter Decontie, my mother's younger brother. "We also do one before we start, asking the Creator and the maple trees for a good harvest." He conducts both ceremonies in the Anishinabe language. After the acknowledgments, elders and schoolchildren enjoy a meal of baked beans and bannock (home-baked bread) dipped in maple syrup. As my mother eats, she remembers the smoky taste of Uncle John's syrup and smiles, happy that maple syruping is still a Kitigan Zibi tradition.

—Millie Knapp

≈ Millie Knapp's mother, Mary Ann Miller (Anishinabe).

Millie Knapp (Anishinabe/Tuscarora) is the president of Knapp Publishing and Knapp Media, Inc. She is the managing editor of *American Indian,* the National Museum of the American Indian's magazine. She holds a master's degree in American Studies from the University of Buffalo (SUNY) with a focus on American Indian women.

MAPLE SYRUP PIE

||| Cree, Assiniboine, and Anishinabe people of central Canada have prepared a form of this pie for centuries. It is quite sweet and very rich. A thin slice accompanied by sliced ripe pears or roasted chestnuts makes a fine and satisfying finale. ||| SERVES 6 TO 8

CRUST
1 cup whole wheat flour

1/4 teaspoon salt

1/4 cup vegetable shortening

1 1/2 to 2 tablespoons ice water

FILLING
1/4 cup unbleached all-purpose flour

1 egg

1/2 cup milk or water

1 cup pure maple syrup

2 tablespoons unsalted butter, at room temperature

To prepare the crust, combine the flour and salt in a bowl and stir with a wooden spoon to mix evenly. Add the shortening and cut into the flour with the tines of a folk until a coarse meal forms. Sprinkle 1 1/2 tablespoons of the water over the mixture and work in with your hands. Add water as necessary to form a firm, shapeable dough. Pat the dough into a disk and smooth the sides. Cover with a kitchen towel and refrigerate for at least 20 minutes or overnight.

Preheat the oven to 400°F. Remove the dough from the refrigerator and leave at room temperature for 5 minutes. Lightly flour a work surface. Sprinkle some flour over the dough and dust a rolling pin with flour. Roll the dough out to an 11-inch round. Transfer the dough to a 9-inch pie pan and press into the bottom and sides. Cut off any excess dough and crimp the edges. Prick the bottom of the shell lightly with the tines of a fork, without piercing all the way through. Place in the oven and bake for 7 to 10 minutes, until golden brown. Remove from the oven and allow to cool completely before filling.

To prepare the filling, place the flour in a heavy saucepan. In a bowl, beat the egg with a whisk. Add the milk and syrup to the egg and whisk well. Add the egg mixture to the flour, beating with a wooden spoon to combine well. Place the pan over medium heat and cook, stirring constantly, for 10 to 15 minutes, until thickened and smooth. Remove from the heat and stir in the butter. Pour the custard into the pie shell and allow to cool at room temperature. Refrigerate for at least 4 hours or overnight before serving. Bring to room temperature before serving.

CHAPTER NINE

BEVERAGES

≈ Zuni polychrome water jar, circa 1875. Ojo Caliente, New Mexico. (22/7879)

The beverages that Native people consume today are similar to those their early ancestors enjoyed. Chocolate, herb teas, cranberry juice, and even soft drinks such as Coca-Cola are derived from indigenous foods.

The Ojibwe of the Great Lakes region made many teas from fresh and dried leaves as well as the twigs of some plants. Whether using leaves or twigs, they fashioned a bundle with a thin strip of basswood bark to fit the size of the pot. In some cases, strips of the same wood as the twigs were used. You can try this method if the materials are available, or simply steep and strain the tea with a tea strainer. A number of teas were made from bark. One tea was made from the inner bark of the elm tree, another from the bark of wild roses.

NAVAJO TEA |||

This tea is cultivated in the American Southwest. Gather Navajo tea (*Thelesperma megapotamicum*) plants before or during flowering. Snap off the stems above the roots and then break the stems to fit your pot. This plant is called *cota* in Pueblo communities. ||| SERVES 4

1 quart water

1 (4 by 2½-inch) bundle Navajo tea

Honey (optional)

In a saucepan, bring the water to a boil over high heat. Drop the bundle of Navajo tea into the pan and decrease the heat to low. Steep for 8 to 10 minutes, until the tea reaches the desired strength. Strain the tea into warm mugs or tea cups and stir in the honey. Serve at once.

YERBA MATÉ |||

Yerba maté (pronounced *mah tay*) is a very popular drink in southern Brazil, Paraguay, Uruguay, and Argentina. *Maté* refers to the original gourd that was hollowed out to serve as a drinking vessel. Maté also refers to the beverage, which is made from the dried leaves of a plant indigenous to Paraguay and other parts of South America. The drink is served in decorative matés with a *bombilla*, or sipping straw, which allows one to sip the beverage without ingesting the tea leaves. The tea tastes of cedar, with a mild, smoky herbaciousness, and can be found at health food stores. You may choose to sweeten your maté and perhaps add a touch of milk, but be aware that it is frowned upon by true *materos!* ||| SERVES 4

4 cups water

1 cup yerba maté

In a saucepan, bring the water to a boil over high heat. Divide the yerba maté among matés, or mugs, and pour in enough water to just moisten. Let the yerba maté stand for 3 to 4 minutes. Add enough water to fill each mug to three-quarters full. Sip the maté through a bombilla, or a regular straw, or strain into fresh hot mugs with a tea strainer. Serve at once.

CHIPPEWA CHILLED MAPLE SYRUP BEVERAGE ||| This

drink is a treat for the diverse peoples who live in the Great Lakes region, where box elders (a type of maple) and

sugar maples grow in abundance. The refreshing cooler is a great way to use up the last bit of maple syrup in your jug.

Photographed opposite with Chicha Morada (page 195). ||| SERVES 4

4 cups water

About 1 cup pure maple syrup or box elder
    syrup

Ice (optional)

Mint leaves, for garnish

Combine the water and syrup in a pitcher and stir well. Taste and add more syrup if desired. Place ice in 4 chilled glasses, and pour in the beverage. Garnish with the mint leaves. Serve at once.

LABRADOR TEA ||| Native communities throughout the northern United States and Canada

make use of the aromatic leaves of Labrador tea, which is also known as marsh tea because its bushes grow in low wet

areas of northern forests. The tea is a good source of vitamin C. ||| SERVES 4

1 cup Labrador tea leaves

4 cups water

1/3 cup maple sugar or syrup (optional)

In a saucepan, combine the leaves and water and bring to a boil over high heat. Decrease the heat to low. Steep for about 15 minutes, until the tea reaches the desired strength. Add the sugar and stir until dissolved. Strain the tea into hot mugs or tea cups and serve at once.

CHOKECHERRY TEA: Replace the Labrador tea leaves with 1 cup chokecherry twigs without leaves. Thin strips of chokecherry bark are acceptable to bundle the twigs.

RED RASPBERRY TEA: Replace the Labrador tea leaves with 1 cup red raspberry tendril tips without leaves.

SNOWBERRY TEA: Replace the Labrador tea leaves with 1 cup creeping snowberry leaves.

WILD CHERRY TEA: Replace the Labrador tea leaves with 1 cup wild cherry twigs without leaves. Thin strips of wild cherry bark are acceptable to bundle the twigs.

CHICHA MORADA (ANDEAN PURPLE CORN DRINK)

||| The principal ingredient in this delicious and striking beverage is purple corn (*maíz morado*), found mainly in Peru (and online at www.spiceworlds.com or at Latin American markets). The kernels are too firm and woody to be eaten and are grown only for this beverage and a type of dessert pudding. In pre-Hispanic times, *chicha* was a corn beer fermented by the Inka. While fermented chicha is still produced today, Peruvians often prefer this simpler nonalcoholic version served over ice. ||| Like most of the recipes in this book, this one has many variations. Because this drink is so satisfying, try this simple recipe first and then experiment with subtle variations, adding seasonal fruits or flavorings. Some people like to add dried fruits to the chicha when brewing the base. Others like to dice fresh fruits (apple and pineapple are two good choices) into the strained chicha to be nibbled while drinking. ||| Photographed with Chippewa Chilled Maple Syrup Beverage, see page 193. ||| SERVES 6

2 ears dried purple corn

2 quarts cold water

1 apple, coarsely chopped

2 whole cloves

3-inch stick cinnamon

1/4 cup honey

3 cups pineapple peel, or 2 cups pineapple flesh

Juice of 2 key limes

In a pot, combine the corn, water, apple, cloves, cinnamon stick, honey, and pineapple peel over high heat. Bring to a full boil, and then decrease the heat to medium. Simmer very lightly for about 20 minutes, until the corn is tender. Cover, remove from the heat, and steep in the pot for 1 hour.

Add the lime juice and stir well. Pass through a fine-mesh sieve and discard the solids. Place the chicha in a pitcher and refrigerate until chilled. Serve very cold over ice. Sweeten with additional honey if desired.

FRESH CORN CHICHA: Replace the dried corn with 2 pounds fresh purple corn. Remove the husks and silk from the cobs. Place the cobs in a pot with 2 quarts water over high heat. Bring to a boil and then decrease the heat to achieve a gentle simmer. Add the apple, cloves, cinnamon stick, honey, and pineapple peel. Cook for 40 to 50 minutes, until the kernels begin to burst, and then proceed as directed in the recipe for steeping.

≈ OPPOSITE: Shuar/Achuar women preparing *chicha*, 1935. Oriente, Ecuador. (P12/648)

Native Hospitality

WE COULD SEE THE APRONED HOPI AUNTS working and talking intently in the kitchen as we entered the spotless Kiqötsmovi community hall and nodded hello. They smiled shyly and continued their work and laughter. Tempting smells wafted from a tabletop array of luscious domed fruit pies; steaming stews; razor-thin, brittle, blue-corn *piki* bread; and intricately scored golden yeast rolls.

All of these details stay with me years after a June trip to the Hopi Reservation in northern Arizona. These surprisingly young, traditional Hopi aunts created a grand feast for eight strangers who expected just a simple lunch before returning to our Native American Journalism Association conference in Tempe. I'm no stranger to Indian hospitality, but this generous expression by the relatives of our Hopi tour guide, Ray Coin, left our group nearly speechless. Although the aunts were far too busy in the kitchen to join us for this repast, their delicious food conveyed their warmth and care for their nephew's guests. Something of the powerful spiritual quality of the Hopi mesas was now inside each visitor, including me.

Throughout Indian Country there is a special kind of graciousness proffered by Native peoples. It is far different from the studied but genuine hospitality I knew while growing up in a history-steeped Virginia seaport. While most Indians take their hospitality very seriously and sincerely, it often has a relaxed and casual style about it that invites conversation and making new friends. It's rare to be invited to an Indian home without immediately being offered copious food, even when it's obvious your hosts have very modest means.

At the annual summer Gathering of our eight Potawatomi tribes at the Forest County Potawatomi's northern Wisconsin homeland in the year 2000, huge open tents sheltered us from endless July rains as we feasted on lasagna and other welcome treats provided by the tribe. Yes, in our multicultural society Indians do dish out this Italian version of comfort food. Activities at the gathering—such as dances, tribal language instruction, and meeting our elders—were enhanced by a constant supply of warm food and blessings. A keen observer will notice at such events that the elders are served first and are accorded special care. It was my first visit to another Potawatomi reservation, and my

PHOTO © JOHN HARRINGTON AND SMITHSONIAN INSTITUTION

≈ Hopi women Camelia Secakuku, Verla Dewakuku, and Tanya Mahle make thirty-two apple pies for an annual social dance in the village of Hano, on the Hopi Reservation.

mind was flooded with thoughts. As I looked around the rain-soaked Gathering grounds, I wondered who of these assembled Potawatomis might be related directly to my family. It didn't take long over the three-day Gathering to realize that despite our eight separate tribes and geographic locations, we were all related in a special way.

Another memorable feast was hosted by tribal leaders of the Great Sioux Nation one relatively mild winter night in 1997 in Bismarck, North Dakota. Amid plates of roast bison, our hosts joked about their guests from Washington having the courage to come to North Dakota in the thick of winter. As is customary at nearly all Indian meals, a blessing was offered for all, this time in Lakota.

The seasons in Indian Country came full circle not too long ago with a huge November dinner proffered by the Coeur d'Alene Tribe at their impressive new casino in Worley, Idaho. Our buses from Spokane made the snowy nighttime trip with only a few slips on icy roads before depositing several hundred hungry Indians at the vast hall. The Coeur d'Alene women stood quietly in the background as we eyed the incredible array of food, all made for strangers they likely would never meet again. Venison, antelope, Indian potatoes, root soup, and mouth-puckering huckleberries gave us a native taste of this tribe's homeland and hospitable nature. Such hospitality is a recurring and reassuring story throughout Indian Country.

—Thomas W. Sweeney

≋ Mindy Secakuku (Hopi) displays eighteen apple pies, which are waiting to be baked in a wood-burning adobe oven outside her family's home on the Hopi Reservation.

Thomas W. Sweeney (Citizen Potawatomi) is the public affairs director of the National Museum of the American Indian. He worked previously as the Bureau of Indian Affairs' public affairs director. Sweeney is an enrolled member of the Citizen Potawatomi Nation of Oklahoma and a longstanding member of the Native American Journalists Association. He is gratified to see how the organization is increasingly helping aspiring young Indian journalists enter the field and establish professional careers.

≈ Jamaica (hibiscus) harvest, Santa María Huatulco, Oaxaca, 1997–1998.

HOT CHOCOLATE ||| A beverage similar to this hot chocolate probably was served to Aztec royalty. The drink was poured from one container to another to form a frothy top, which was most prized by those fortunate enough to imbibe the revered drink. Today, Zapotec women in the Mexican state of Oaxaca spin wooden bobbins to froth hot chocolate. ||| MAKES 4 CUPS

2 ounces bittersweet chocolate

3 tablespoons honey

4 cups milk

1- to 2-inch piece cinnamon stick, or
   1/4 teaspoon ground cinnamon

Combine the chocolate, honey, milk, and cinnamon in the top of a double boiler or a saucepan set over a larger pan of water. Place over medium-high heat. Stir occasionally for about 15 minutes, until the chocolate is melted and the mixture heated through. Pour the hot chocolate into warm mugs, discard the cinnamon stick, and serve at once.

AGUA DE JAMAICA ||| This fragrant drink made from hibiscus flowers (called *jamaica* in Spanish) is unusual, refreshing, and delicious. It can usually be found among the colorful beverages on display throughout the market stalls of Mexico. It is a nice accompaniment to any of the Mexican recipes in this book. You can find the flowers in Latin American markets. ||| SERVES 8

1 cup dried hibiscus flowers, washed
   and drained

8 cups water

1/2 cup sugar

Combine the flowers, water, and sugar in a saucepan over high heat. Bring to a boil and then immediately remove from the heat. Pour into a glass or plastic pitcher. Allow to cool completely at room temperature, and then refrigerate for at least 5 hours or overnight. Strain and serve in chilled glasses with ice.

BASIC
COOKING
METHODS &
PREPARATIONS

≈ Seneca boy in a longhouse kitchen, 1907. (N2635)

Most of the recipes in this book may be prepared in standard cookware on an electric, gas, or propane stove. For some recipes, an indoor grill or an outdoor fire pit or barbecue is the preferred way to impart natural flavors to the foods. It's best if your grill or barbecue is fitted with a lid, although in many cases natural wrappers are suggested, as they are often the most effective and economical means of achieving delicious results. For those living in regions where it is not practical to use a barbecue, alternative techniques are provided to help you produce the intended flavors.

Don't worry about being strict with the recipes in this book. Cooking techniques for the cuisines of the Americas reflect the season, region, and, above all, the cook's practical—or whimsical—approach. Once you have mastered a recipe, let your own tastes be your guide, and improvise freely.

BRAISING TIPS

Braised foods are succulent and tender, savory and satisfying, perfect for an evening meal any time of the year. It is likely that Native people developed the technique of braising through trial and error before arriving at a method that has long served them well. With the few basic tips provided here, anyone can enjoy this convenient, economical, practical, and easy technique for preparing meats and vegetables.

The primary difference between braising and boiling is that braised foods are browned prior to the addition of liquid, and the amount of liquid is generally less than that used to boil. Braising yields a significantly richer and thicker broth than do other methods.

The recipes for Braised American Buffalo (page 76), Braised Lamb Shanks (page 83), and Great Basin–Style Braised Rabbit (page 84) all begin with seasoning the foods, browning them over high heat, and then adding their respective liquids, which have been heated first in a separate pan, speeding the process. After adding the hot liquid to your braising pan, make sure to bring the mixture to a full boil before covering. Be sure that the lid is tight-fitting. If it doesn't fit tightly, simply cover the inside of the lid with a piece of foil and loosely fold it around the rim to extend the lid.

Using the proper pan for braising can make the difference between a pleasurable cooking experience or a difficult and dirty affair. Select an enameled cast-iron casserole dish or a glazed ceramic casserole dish with a tight-fitting lid. These types of braising dishes will produce better results, not only because the heat is distributed more evenly, but also because these materials are very easy to clean.

SMOKING TIPS

Native peoples attempting to dry their winter stores of foods often required heat beyond that available from the sun. In regions with climates that approximate present-day New England or the rugged coast of Tierra del Fuego, it often took days to dry whole or large pieces of fish, meats, nuts, vegetables, or fruits. Smoking foods became a practical solution.

Smoked foods gently remind the palate of some of the earliest aromas and flavors known to humans. There are two methods for smoking—cold-smoking and hot-smoking. The method used by early Native peoples is referred to today as cold-smoking. This method of preservation requires much time and attention. The principle of cold-smoking is to dry out the foods with minimal heat, below 90°F. While advanced cooks may undertake this form of smoking, the focus in this book is on hot-smoking foods.

Hot-smoking allows cooks to cater to their own special tastes in their choices of woods and flavorings. Hot-smoking may be accomplished by simply adding some herbs to a fire beneath the cooking foods. Some smoking takes place when foods are placed on the grill of a broiler or barbecue.

Vegetables cooked on a grill have a gentle smoke flavor, imparted by allowing the skin to char slightly. Tomatoes, squash, corn, and chiles are all superb when cooked this way. Wrapping foods in moist leaves or greens allows them to smolder and steam and may also impart a smoked flavor. This type of smoking is used in preparing dishes such as Imu-Style Salmon (page 131) and Yucatán-Style Pork (page 89).

Hot-smoking is easily incorporated into most home cooks' repertoires. It is simple to accomplish with a minimum of equipment. A small electric smoker may be purchased at any good outdoors store. Any barbecue grill with a lid can be used to smoke, or a simple indoor smoker may be fashioned from a braising pan.

To convert a barbecue with a tight-fitting cover into a smoker, remove the grill rack and mound a small portion of coals to one side of the barbecue. Ignite the coals and allow them to burn down to embers. Soak hickory, apple, or cherry wood chips in water to cover for about 15 minutes. Drain the wood chips thoroughly and place them on the coal embers, leaving about half of the embers exposed. Add more wood chips if necessary to keep the embers smoking. Place the grill rack in its highest setting. Place meats, fish, poultry, or vegetables on the grill rack, away from direct heat. Poultry should be cut into serving pieces and other foods should not exceed 1 inch in thickness. You should expect to get about 20 minutes of smoke time with this method. Generally speaking, foods smoked this way will require additional cooking. You can refuel the barbecue for another round of smoking or finish the cooking in the oven. Soft foods such as summer squash and tomatoes and small fish such as herring and trout may finish cooking in just one smoking session.

Hot-smoking may be done indoors over an electric burner, but great care must be taken to provide adequate ventilation in the kitchen. To prepare a stovetop smoker, place some soaked wood chips in an empty tin; a very clean tuna can works well for this. Place the chip-filled tin in a heavy-bottomed braising pan large enough to hold the foods to be smoked. Place a cake rack over the fuel tin. Place the prepared foods on the rack and cover the top, sealing loosely with aluminum foil. Turn on the burner to medium heat. When smoke appears, gradually reduce the heat to the lowest possible setting while smoke remains visible. Take care not to overcook your foods. Ten to fifteen minutes is generally adequate to impart a pleasant flavor. This assembly works well for thin cuts of meat and fish or for small whole vegetables. Smoke the foods until done or until smoke is no longer visible.

CHILES

Chiles are an excellent source of vitamin C. The seeds of chiles contain the heat. The seeds are generally removed before chiles are used, although some recipes (*moles,* for example) call for the seeds to be left in. After trying some of the recipes in this book, you may choose to leave some of the seeds in the chiles for extra heat the next time you prepare them.

Chiles can be volatile. Although hands don't typically react to them, the oils in chile flesh can cause pain and swelling when they come into contact with skin. Therefore, wash your hands immediately after handling and preparing both fresh and dried chiles, as the oils are easily transferred from your hands. You may choose to wear nonlatex gloves when handling chiles to avoid the possibility of residual contact.

To prepare unpeeled chiles, rinse and dry the chiles and then remove the stems (except with recipes that specify otherwise). Split the chiles open using a sharp knife, and, using the tip of the knife, scrape out the seeds and cut away the white membrane.

To peel chiles, place them over direct heat. A broiler, barbecue, or open gas burner works well. Cook for 4 to 5 minutes, turning several times, to char evenly. Direct flame will cause a visible charring, which imparts a sensational flavor to the chiles.

Alternatively, fry the chiles in a little corn oil over medium-high heat, turning to blister as evenly as possible. Frying produces results similar to that of a traditional *comal,* a Mexican ceramic cooking surface.

Try to accomplish the charring or blistering as quickly as possible. The flavor and texture of the chiles are more intense and appealing if the chiles are not overcooked in the peeling process. After charring or blistering the chiles, place them in a plastic bag and let steam for about 5 minutes. Using a paring knife, scrape away the skin from stem to tip. Do not rinse the chiles under any circumstance as this greatly diminishes the terrific flavor developed by the charring or blistering process.

To remove the seeds for stuffed chile rellenos, as with Roasted Chile Poblano Rellenos (page 8), make an incision in the chile with a sharp knife to form a pocket from stem to tip. Gently open the pocket and cut the seed pod from the stem, leaving the stem intact. Cut close to the stem, taking care not to cut through the chile. Remove the seeds without tearing or splitting the flesh. Use a spoon to scoop out stubborn seeds.

TOMATOES

One key aspect of American cookery that clearly separates it from European cookery is the basic processing of tomatoes before they are used in recipes. Europeans blanch, shock, peel, and seed tomatoes prior to most preparations. Indigenous Americans opt for sealing in the flavor and perhaps enhancing it by first cooking them in or over direct heat—be it buried in ash, directly over a fire, on a *comal* (a Mexican ceramic cooking surface), or fried in oil. The flavor developed by roasting tomatoes over a fire provides the soul of the dish. Preparing a salsa after blanching the tomatoes produces a sauce without soul—a sauce that is not American, a sauce that must be reduced (with a radical loss of nutrients), as is the practice in Europe.

Tomatoes are at their best when plucked ripe from the vine. While it may be necessary to refrigerate tomatoes after they have been prepared in various ways, whole, fresh tomatoes should never be refrigerated. They are the most flavorful at room temperature, or heated. Freshly picked ripe tomatoes often can be peeled without any advance preparation. Short of that, and to impart a delicious if subtle smoky flavor, follow the grill method below.

To roast or grill tomatoes, first lightly score an X into the flower end of the tomato with the tip of a sharp knife. Cut the tomatoes in half horizontally and place them with the cut side up on the grill of a hot barbecue or broiler. Let the skins char, then transfer to a plate and cool slightly. When the tomatoes are cool enough to handle, remove the skins. The juice and seeds may be undesirable to some, but they do provide moisture and nutrients. The tomatoes are now ready to use in recipes.

As an alternative to the grill method, place a little corn oil in a skillet and, over medium-high heat, fry the tomatoes, rolling them with tongs or a fork to blister evenly. Cool slightly to handle. Core and peel the tomatoes.

VEGETABLE STOCK ||| This recipe is a terrific way to use less-than-perfect vegetables. Feel free to substitute seasonal vegetables that are of a similar type or texture to suit the time of year and to reflect the freshest flavors. Beans add depth of flavor and give body to the stock. Use light-colored beans for spring or summer and dark beans and deep-hued root vegetables (with their greens) for wintry versions. ||| MAKES ABOUT 12 CUPS

2 tablespoons corn oil

1 russet or other starchy potato, skin on, coarsely chopped

1/2 small celery root, coarsely chopped

1 white onion, skin on, coarsely chopped

1 ramp, wild onion, or leek, white and green parts, coarsely chopped

2 carrots, peeled and coarsely chopped

2 wild or cultivated celery stalks, coarsely chopped

1 cup coarsely chopped summer squash, with seeds and skin

1/4 cup small white or other small beans

2 bay leaves

1 cup spinach leaves, amaranth leaves or seeds, miner's lettuce, or new nettle tops

3 sage leaves

1/2 bunch parsley

4 cloves garlic

1 teaspoon sea or kosher salt

12 cups water

Heat the oil in a large pot over medium-high heat. Add the potato, celery root, onion, ramp, carrots, celery, and squash. Cook for 7 to 10 minutes, until softened but not browned. Add the beans, bay leaves, spinach, sage, parsley, garlic, salt, and water. Bring to a simmer and then decrease the heat to medium-low to maintain a slow simmer. Cook, stirring occasionally, for 1 hour. Remove from the heat and allow to cool slightly. Pass through a fine-mesh sieve, discarding the solids and capturing the liquid. This stock will keep for 3 to 4 days in the refrigerator and 2 to 3 months in the freezer.

BROWN STOCK |||

Beef bones should be readily available, but you may use a veal shank to replace hard-to-find bones. The calf foot could be replaced by more veal bones or an equal measure of chicken legs or thighs. Keep in mind that many substitutions are possible, as illustrated by the variations below. Keep the bones covered with liquid at all times, keep the temperature constant, and don't allow the stock to boil. Skim the stock regularly to ensure a clear, full flavored stock. ||| MAKES ABOUT 16 CUPS

2 pounds beef bones and trimmings
  (trimmings optional)

2 pounds veal bones and trimmings
  (trimmings optional)

1 calf or pig foot (optional)

1 gallon (16 cups) cold water

1/2 small white onion, coarsely chopped

1/2 small carrot, peeled and coarsely
  chopped

2 tomatoes, coarsely chopped

1 bay leaf

1 small clove garlic

1 sprig thyme

2 sprigs flat-leaf parsley, with stems

Preheat the oven to 400°F. Place the beef and veal bones and calf foot in a heavy roasting pan. Reserve the trimmings. Place in the oven and cook for about 30 minutes, until browned and caramelized. Maintain the oven temperature at 400°F. Transfer the bones to a large soup pot over high heat and add the water. Bring to a simmer and then decrease the heat as necessary to maintain a slow simmer. Skim off the impurities with a slotted spoon as they accumulate. As the liquid evaporates, maintain the water level by adding boiling water.

Place the meat trimmings, onion, carrot, and tomatoes in a roasting pan. Place in the oven and cook for 25 to 30 minutes, until browned. Add the trimmings and vegetables to the soup pot. Place the roasting pan on the stovetop over medium-high heat. Add 2 cups of the simmering broth and deglaze the pan by scraping up the browned bits on the bottom of the pan with a wooden spoon. Pour the deglazed liquid into the soup pot. Add the bay leaf, garlic, thyme, and parsley and simmer for 10 to 12 hours, skimming often. Continue to add water to maintain the liquid level. Remove from the heat and allow to cool slightly. Pass through a fine-mesh sieve, discarding the solids and capturing the liquid. This stock will keep for 5 to 7 days in the refrigerator and 2 to 3 months in the freezer.

CHICKEN, DUCK, OR WILD FOWL BROWN STOCK: Replace the beef bones and trimmings with 3 pounds chicken, duck, or wild fowl bones and trimmings. Decrease the veal bones and trimmings to 1 pound. Decrease the final cooking time to 4 to 5 hours.

LAMB, BISON, GOAT, OR VENISON BROWN STOCK: Replace the beef bones and trimmings with an equal amount of lamb, bison, goat, or venison bones and trimmings. Replace the water with white stock (page 209).

WHITE STOCK

||| Use this stock for all preparations that don't require the body and depth of flavor of brown stock. This stock works well as a liquid for steaming wild rice, for cooking beans, or for making thick soups containing vegetables and meat trimmings. ||| **MAKES ABOUT 16 CUPS**

2 pounds veal bones and trimmings

2 pounds chicken, rabbit, duck, or partridge bones and trimmings

½ pound chicken giblets

1 gallon (16 cups) cold water

1 teaspoon sea or kosher salt

½ small white onion, coarsely chopped

½ small carrot, peeled and coarsely chopped

½ celery stalk, coarsely chopped

½ small leek, coarsely chopped

1 bay leaf

1 whole clove

1 sprig thyme

2 sprigs flat-leaf parsley, with stems

Place the bones, trimmings, giblets, water, and salt in a large pot over high heat. Bring just to a simmer and then decrease the heat as necessary to maintain a slow simmer. Skim off the impurities with a slotted spoon as they accumulate. Add the onion, carrot, celery, leek, bay leaf, clove, thyme, and parsley. Continue cooking at a low simmer, skimming as necessary, for 4 to 5 hours. As the liquid evaporates, maintain the water level by adding boiling water. Remove from the heat and allow to cool slightly. Pass through a fine-mesh sieve, discarding the solids and capturing the liquid. This stock will keep for 1 week in the refrigerator and 2 to 3 months in the freezer.

CREMA

||| *Crema,* an easy-to-prepare cultured cream, is an essential accompaniment to many regional Mexican dishes. North Americans generally substitute sour cream for crema, but sour cream will curdle when cooked. To use in cooked sauces, apply gradual, even heat to the sauce containing crema. If the sauce requires reduction, do this before adding the crema. ||| **MAKES 2½ CUPS**

1 pint heavy cream

½ cup buttermilk

Place the cream and buttermilk in a bowl and whisk to blend thoroughly. Transfer to a glass or ceramic vessel and cover with a linen towel or cheesecloth. Place the crema in a warm place (about 110°F). The stovetop (not on a burner) or near a water heater are usually good places. Let sit, undisturbed, for 6 to 8 hours. Remove the towel and stir gently with a wooden spoon. Cover tightly with plastic wrap and place in the refrigerator for at least 12 hours to complete the culture.

ANNATTO OIL ||| Annatto seeds are used extensively throughout South America and in Mexico's Yucatán Peninsula, where they are the basis of a seasoning paste called *achiote*. Annatto is used principally for its brilliant orange to red color, but it also contributes a subtle, background flavor that is truly unique. When combined with the toasted spices and flavorings of its Maya region of origin, it helps transfer the flavors to the foods being marinated. Annatto seeds can be found at health food stores or at Latin American markets. Paprika oil (below) can be substituted in any recipe calling for annatto oil. ||| MAKES 1 CUP

1 cup corn oil

1/2 cup annatto seeds

Place the oil and annatto seeds in a saucepan over medium heat, stirring often. When heated, annatto seeds quickly turn a brilliant reddish orange color. Heat for about 10 minutes and remove the pan from the burner. Let the seeds steep for about 30 minutes. Strain the oil through cheesecloth, discard the seeds, and allow the oil to cool. Store tightly covered in the refrigerator for up to 2 months.

PAPRIKA OIL ||| This oil is used to cook various dishes throughout Chile and may be used as a substitute for annatto oil, although the flavor is quite different. ||| MAKES 1 CUP

1 cup corn oil

1/2 cup sweet paprika

Place the oil and paprika in a saucepan over medium heat, stirring often. Heat for about 10 minutes and remove the pan from the heat. Let the mixture steep for about 30 minutes. Use at once or allow to cool completely. Store tightly covered in the refrigerator for up to 2 months.

GLOSSARY

This list provides the origins and sources for some of the more unusual ingredients used in this book. Common names, indigenous names, and area of origin are provided when known.

ACHIOTE PASTE. Also called *condimento achiote,* this is one of a multitude of Maya pastes, or *recados,* that Mesoamerican cooks use to flavor their food, mainly meats. The red paste is made principally from crushed annatto seed with the addition of garlic, fresh herbs, and seasonings. It is often thinned with citrus juices to a spreadable consistency, then used as a meat marinade. This is the flavoring for Yucatán-Style Pork (page 89).

ANNATTO. The annatto plant is grown in warm, tropical climates in North and South America, parts of Mexico, the Caribbean, and South Africa. The dried layer of material that encases the seeds of the annatto plant is ground to a paste, called *achiote,* which is used throughout the Caribbean for various flavorings. Throughout South America, the seeds are steeped in oil to extract flavor and color. For ease of preparation, choose ground annatto powder, which is aromatic and brilliant in color. Whole seeds may be used; however, they are very hard and difficult to grind without a coarse mortar and pestle. Annatto seeds and powder can be found at health food stores, at Latin American markets, or in the Latin American section of most supermarkets.

BANANA LEAVES. Leaves from the banana plant are harvested, folded into square shapes, and packaged and sold in Asian or Latin markets, or in ethnic foods sections of large supermarkets (often they are sold frozen). Banana leaves impart a subtle anise-like flavor to foods. Alternatives include green leek leaves, ti leaves, or Swiss chard leaves. Aluminum foil or parchment paper provide flavorless alternatives.

BISON (BUFFALO). Bison is a lean meat with much less cholesterol than beef and has nutritional value that exceeds beef. For thousands of years, Native people of the Plains hunted the North American bison, or buffalo. The Plains peoples' survival depended on the buffalo, and they adapted numerous hunting techniques to obtain their livelihood. The most sophisticated technique was the buffalo jump. This form of harvesting bison was a communal effort that included a network of drive lanes used to gather herds and direct them to cliffs, over which they would jump to their deaths. Near the bottom of the jump site, families camped while they processed the animals. Meat was sliced into thin strips and hung on racks to dry in the sun. Large leg bones were pulverized to remove the nutritious marrow, and broken bones were boiled to render oil used for cooking and burned for light. The boiling was achieved by throwing red-hot rocks into hide-lined pits filled with water.

While some of the buffalo meat was eaten fresh by roasting, boiling, or braising, much of the meat obtained from the buffalo was processed into pemmican. To make pemmican, oil and marrow rendered from the bones were pounded together with dried meat and sometimes berries. Pemmican is a very nutritious staple food that can be preserved for years.

CANELA. This variety of cinnamon is made from the bark of a tree that originally grew in Sri Lanka and now also is cultivated in Mexico. This variety has a milder, softer taste than the cinnamon most common in North America. Use less of the latter when substituting.

CATTAILS. The pollen, roots, and stalks of this reed-like marsh plant all can be used as foods. In the spring, cattail pollen is harvested by tapping pollen-rich cattail heads into a bag. In the fall and winter, the bulbous root is peeled, grated, dried, and ground into flour. Use both pollen and flour in tandem with other flours in breads and cakes. Since cattails grow everywhere in North America, harvesting them is not difficult.

CHILES. Chiles, which are grown all over the world, were gathered in wild form in Mexico as early as circa 7000 B.C. and were being cultivated there before 3500 B.C. The word *chile* is derived from the Nahuatl language. Following are some commonly used types. They can be found in most supermarkets or Latin markets.

Aji. *Aji* is the name in Peru, Chile, and Ecuador for small, red or green hot chiles that grow throughout the region. Aji are often combined with onions and salt to make a unique condiment. Any small, hot, fresh chiles or dried, crushed chiles can be substituted for aji.

Anaheim. Developed in California around 1900 for a newly established cannery in Anaheim, these chiles range in color from pale to yellowish green. These chiles can be mild, with floral overtones. Roasting improves the flavor immensely. Select firm, shiny chiles with supple stems.

Cayenne. Cayenne powder is made from the ground seed of the cayenne chile, which has thin, pointed pods that are 4 to 12 inches long. These chiles are intensely hot and are used fresh or dried. The word *cayenne* probably came from the Tupí-Guaraní language, which is spoken in the Amazon Basin.

Habañero. These chiles may have originated in Cuba, as the name refers to Havana. Habañeros are very hot, ranging in color from red, yellow, and orange to green. Select brilliantly colored chiles that are firm, with supple rather than dried stems.

Jalapeño. A hot chile, named for the town of Jalapa in Veracruz state, Mexico, the jalapeño may be used fresh or dried. Dried and smoked jalapeños are called chipotle chiles. They have a wrinkled, dark brown skin and a smoky, sweet, slightly chocolatey flavor. You may substitute canned chipotle chiles in adobo (a dark red sauce made from ground chiles, herbs, and vinegar) for smoked jalapeños.

Pasilla. *Pasa* means "raisin" in Spanish, a name that reflects the dark color and wrinkled texture of this relatively mild chile. Select supple, dry chiles that are not brittle and do not crumble when grasped.

Serrano. This hot chile, named for mountain ridges (*serranias*) in Mexico, where it originally grew, is usually eaten while still green, but it can also be smoked and dried.

COLTSFOOT. Found throughout North America, this plant from the daisy family has yellow petals that are used to make a wine and an herbal tea. The ash produced by burning the dry leaves was used as a salt substitute by many indigenous people of North America. Dried coltsfoot leaves can be bought in health food stores. Simply burn them in a pan, allow the ashes to cool, and crumble for use.

MATÉ. *Yerba maté* is a tea made from the dried leaves of a shrub in the holly family, which grows wild near streams and thrives at 1,500 to 2,000 feet above sea level. Maté was popular with the pre-Columbian peoples of Paraguay, Uruguay, Argentina, and Brazil, but it is now cultivated in many tropical countries. Like coffee and tea, maté contains caffeine. It is usually drunk without sugar, although burnt sugar and orange peel are sometimes added.

PLANTAINS. Plantains are widely distributed throughout the tropical regions of the Americas. The unripe fruit is rich in starch and only slightly sweet. Plaintains are larger than their cousin, the banana, and are used like any starchy vegetable. They can be baked, roasted, boiled, fried, or added to soups or stews. The plantain can also be dried and powdered.

QUINOA. Quinoa is related to spinach and grows from southern Colombia to northwest Argentina and northern Chile. Quinoa is able to grow at altitudes too high for maize. At the time of the Conquest, quinoa was an important commodity for the Inka and Aztec peoples. The Inka called it "the mother grain." Quinoa has high nutritional value, equal to milk in the quality of its protein. It's considered a complete protein, as it contains all eight amino acids. The grain, which is higher in unsaturated fats and lower in carbohydrates than most grains, is tiny and round and expands to four times its original volume when cooked. The leaves can be eaten as a green vegetable, but care must be taken to wash them first in an alkaline solution to remove the apparently toxic compounds. *Huauzontle* is another species, native to Mexico, which looks like broccoli. Its immature seed heads are eaten whole and also dipped in batter and fried.

SALICORNIA. Also called glasswort, salicornia can be found in estuaries throughout the Americas. The succulents are full of salt and turn a brilliant green when steamed. This lovely plant can be eaten as a snack or used to cover foods for steaming, as with Imu-Style Salmon (page 131). Salicornia also can be added sparingly to seafood stews as a flavoring and vegetable.

TI LEAVES. Used to flavor and steam fish, vegetables, and meats throughout the South Pacific, these beautiful leaves grow to be quite long. Alternatives for ti leaves are the same as for banana leaves.

TOMATILLOS. Tomatillos grow abundantly in Mexico and Guatemala and were a staple in the Aztec and Maya economies. The tomatillo resembles the fruit of the true tomato in its unripe, green state. When ripe it may vary in color from green to yellow to purple. It is sold with husks that must be removed before cooking.

WAPATO. Known to the Dakota as *Pshi tola,* to the Omaha people as *Si,* and to the Pawnee as *kirit,* wapato is found along streams and riverbanks, and in ponds. One identifies the plant by the arrowhead-shaped leaf, which stands up above the water. The root is roasted, peeled, and eaten like a potato, or it can be peeled, sliced, and added to a soup or stew. The taste is similar to that of a potato (perhaps a little mealier), with a nice nutty flavor.

≋ Nez Perce bag woven of natural and dyed cornhusk strips, late 1800s. (13/8632)

Sources

BROKEN ARROW RANCH
104 Highway 27 West
Box 530
Ingram, TX 78025
(800) 962-4263
   Wild boar, antelope, deer; sold at Whole Foods markets

CAJUNGROCER.COM
Corporate Office
208 West Pinhook Road
Lafayette, LA 70503
(888) 272-9347
Fax (337) 264-1366
www.cajungrocer.com
   Frog legs

CANYON WREN RANCH
Navajo-Churro Lamb
92425 East Aravaipa Road
Winkelman, AZ 85292
   Lamb

THE COOKING POST
The Pueblo of Santa Ana
2 Dove Road
Bernalillo, New Mexico 87004
(888) 867-5198
(505) 771-8318
Fax (505) 867-3395
info@cookingpost.com
www.cookingpost.com
   Hominy, wild rice

DENNIS BANKS & CO., LTD
P.O. Box 134
Federal Dam, MN 56641
(218) 654-5885
Fax (218) 654-5886
www.dbcnaturalfoods.com
   Wild rice and maple syrup produced by indigenous people

ECOFISH
78 Market Street
Portsmouth, NH 03801
(603) 430-0101
(877) 214-FISH
Fax (603) 430-9929
www.ecofish.com
   Fish and shellfish, harvested in environmentally
   responsible ways

GOURMET IMPORTS
128 East Wood Drive
Phoenix, AZ 85022
(602) 271-6335
   Wild game, wild game birds, frog legs

INTERTRIBAL BISON COOPERATIVE
1560 Concourse Drive
Rapid City, SD 57709
(605) 394-9730
Fax (605) 394-7742
itbc@enetis.net
   Bison meat

JAMESTOWN SEAFOOD
3830 West Sequim Road
Sequim, WA 98382
(360) 683-2482
(360) 683-1028
seafood@mail.olympus.net
   Dungeness crab

NATIVE SEEDS/SEARCH
526 North 4th Avenue
Tucson, AZ 85705-8450
(520) 622-5561
Fax (520) 622-5591
info@nativeseeds.org
www.nativeseeds.org
   Sonoran mesquite flour, various cornmeals, chiles, beans

PERUANITO'S INC.
2051 West Warner Road
Chandler, AZ 85244
(480) 821-9498
　　Purple corn, quinoa

PRIMA GOURMET
(360) 882-1209
sales@primagourmet.com
www.primagourmet.com
　　Wild mushrooms, huckleberries, fiddlehead ferns, ramps,
　　salicornia (sea beans)

RED CORN NATIVE FOODS
13109 West 76th St.
Lenexa, KS 66216
(913) 248-1980
Fax (913) 248-0553
info@redcorn.com
　　Hominy

SHEPHERD'S LAMB
P.O. Box 307
Tierra Amarilla, NM 87575
(505) 588-7792
shepherd@rioarriba.com
　　Lamb

TANIOKA'S SEAFOODS & CATERING
Farrington Highway
Waipahu, Oahu, HI 94093
(808) 671-3779
　　Hawaiian foods such as dried seaweed and fresh
　　and frozen fish

THE WILD GOURMET
Lee Gray
P.O. Box 6
Depoe Bay, OR 97341
(541) 996-3797
leegray@charter.net
　　Cattail products, huckleberries, salicornia (sea beans),
　　nodding onions, coltsfoot, miner's lettuce, nettles,
　　fiddlehead ferns, wild mushrooms, ramps, licorice fern
　　root, wild mustard, wild mint, wild gingerroot, wild berries

BIBLIOGRAPHY

Anderson, Jean, and Yeffe Kimball. *The Art of American Indian Cooking.* New York: Doubleday, 1965.

Batdorf, Carol. *Northwest Native Harvest.* Surrey, British Columbia: Hancock House Publishers, 1990.

Bayless, Rick, with Deann Groen Bayless. *Authentic Mexican.* New York: William Morrow and Company, 1987.

Bishop Museum. "Plants of the Past—Meakanu o Kahiko." http://www.bishopmuseum.org/exhibits/1995/pastExhibits/hawaiilo/hawgard.html.

Ciment, James, with Ronald LaFrance. *Scholastic Encyclopedia of the North American Indian.* New York: Scholastic, 1996.

Coe, Sophie D. *America's First Cuisines.* Austin, Texas: University of Texas Press, 1994.

Coe, Sophie D., and Michael D. Coe. *The True History of Chocolate.* New York: Thames & Hudson, 1996.

Cook, Katsi. "Berry Plants for Women's Nutrition & Medicine." *Indigenous Woman Magazine,* no. IV (1992).

Council of Indian Nations. "Southwest Indian History: 300 BC: Hohokam." http://www.cinprograms.org/history/hohokam.html.

Cox, Beverly, and Martin Jacobs. *Spirit of the Harvest: North American Indian Cooking.* New York: Stewart, Tabori, and Chang, 1991.

———. *Spirit of the Earth: Native Cooking from Latin America.* New York: Stewart, Tabori, and Chang, 2001.

Crop Plant Resources. "Quinoa." New Mexico State University Molecular Biology Program. http://www.nmsu.edu/~molbio/plant/quinoa.html.

Cunningham, Marion. *The Breakfast Book.* New York: Alfred A. Knopf, 1987.

Davidson, Alan. *The Oxford Companion to Food.* New York: Oxford University Press, 1999.

de Benitez, Ana M. *Pre-Hispanic Cooking/Cocina prehispanica.* D.F., Mexico: Ediciones Euroamericanas Klaus Thiele, 1974.

Densmore, Frances. *How Indians Use Wild Plants for Food.* Toronto: General Publishing Company, 1974.

Erickson, Clark L. "An Artificial Landscape—Scale Fishery in the Bolivian Amazon." *Nature* 408 (9 November 2000): 190–93.

Everson, Gene, and Lynn Scheu. "The Shell Indians." The Conchologists of America and Academy of Natural Sciences Philadelphia. http://coa.acnatsci.org/conchnet/indians.html.

Gilmore, Melvin R. *Uses of Plants by the Indians of the Missouri River Region.* Lincoln: University of Nebraska Press, 1977.

Gunther, Erna. *Ethnobotany of Western Washington: The Knowledge and Use of Indigenous Plants by Native Americans,* rev. ed. Seattle: University of Washington Press, 1973.

Harbo, Rick M. *The Edible Seashore.* Surrey, British Columbia: Hancock House Publishers, 1949.

Hatch, Peter J. "Strawberries: 'Arcadian Dainties with a True Paradisaical Flavor.'" *Twinleaf Journal* (1997).

Heiser, Charles B., Jr. *Seed to Civilization: The Story of Food.* Cambridge: Harvard University Press, 1954.

Hughes, Phyllis. *Pueblo Indian Cookbook.* Santa Fe: Museum of New Mexico Press, 1972.

Hungry Wolf, Adolf. *Teachings of Nature.* Summertown, Tenn.: Book Publishing Co., 1992.

Josephy, Alvin M., Jr. *500 Nations: An Illustrated History of North American Indians.* New York: Alfred A. Knopf, 1994.

Karoff, Barbara. *South American Cooking.* Berkeley, Calif.: Addison-Wesley, 1991.

Kavasch, E. Barrie. *Enduring Harvests: Native American Foods and Festivals for Every Season.* Old Saybrook, Conn.: Globe Pequot Press, 1995.

Keegan, Marcia. *Southwest Indian Cookbook.* Santa Fe: Clear Light, 1987.

Kennedy, Diana. *The Art of Mexican Cooking.* New York: Bantam Books, 1989.

———. *Mexican Regional Cooking.* New York: Harper Colophon Books, 1978.

Kiple, Kenneth F., and Kriemhild Conneè Ornelas. *The Cambridge World History of Food.* Cambridge: Cambridge University Press, 2000.

Knife River Indian Villages National Historic Site. Teacher's Guide: "Subsistence." http://www.nps.gov/knri/teach/subsist.htm.

Kopper, Phillip. *The Smithsonian Book of North American Indians.* Washington, D.C.: Smithsonian Books, 1986.

Kozloff, Eugene N. *Plants and Animals of the Pacific Northwest.* Seattle: University of Washington Press, 1976.

Kurlansky, Mark. *Salt.* New York: Penguin Books, 2002.

Leonard, Jonathan Norton, and the Editors of Time-Life Books. *Latin American Cooking.* New York: Time-Life Books, 1968.

Lutins, Allen. "Prehistoric Fishweirs in Eastern North America." Master's thesis, New York State University at Binghamton, 1992.

Mahoney, Russ. *Why Wild Edibles?* Seattle: Pacific Search, 1975.

Nabhan, Gary Paul. *Enduring Seeds.* Tucson: University of Arizona Press, 1989.

Native American Ethnobotany: A Database of Foods, Drugs, Dyes, and Fibers of Native American Peoples, Derived from Plants. University of Michigan—Dearborn College. http://herb.umd.umich.edu.

National Research Council. *Lost Crops of the Incas: Little-Known Plants of the Andes with Promise for Worldwide Cultivation.* Washington, D.C.: National Academy Press, 1989.

Ortiz, Elisabeth Lambert. *The Book of Latin American Cooking.* New York: Alfred A. Knopf, 1979.

———. *The Complete Book of Caribbean Cooking.* New York: Ballantine Books, 1973.

Palazuelos, Susanna, Marilyn Tausend, and Ignacio Urquiza. *Mexico the Beautiful Cookbook: Authentic Recipes from the Regions of Mexico.* San Francisco: HarperCollins, 1991.

Poehiman, Charles H., ed. "Foods of the Desert Cultures." Chap. 4 in *Know Your Nevada Indians.* Carson City: Nevada State Department of Education, 1973.

Quintana, Patricia. *The Taste of Mexico.* New York: Stewart, Tabori, and Chang, 1986.

Ruby, Robert H., and John A. Brown. *A Guide to the Indian Tribes of the Pacific Northwest.* Norman, Okla.: University of Oklahoma Press, 1986.

Stark, Raymond. *Guide to Indian Herbs.* Blaine, Wash.: Hancock House Publishers, 1981.

Steward, Julian, and Louis C. Faron. *Native Peoples of South America.* New York: McGraw-Hill, 1959.

Stewart, Hilary. *Indian Fishing: Early Methods on the Northwest Coast.* Seattle: University of Washington Press, 1977.

Tower, Jeremiah. *New American Classics.* New York: Harper and Row, 1986.

Turner, Nancy Chapman. *Food Plants of Coastal Peoples.* Vancouver: University of British Columbia Press in collaboration with the Royal British Columbia Museum, 1995.

U.S. Department of Agriculture Natural Resources Conservation Service Plants Database. http://plants.usda.gov.

Ulmer, Mary, and Samuel Beck. *Cherokee Cooklore.* Cherokee, N.C.: Museum of the Cherokee Indian, 1951.

Umaña-Murray, Mirtha. *Three Generations of Chilean Cuisine.* Los Angeles: Lowell House, 1997.

Underwood, Thomas B., and J. Sharpe, eds. *American Indian Cooking and Herb Lore.* Cherokee, N.C., 1973.

Waldman, Carl. *Atlas of the North American Indian.* New York: Facts on File, 1985.

Weatherford, Jack. *Native Roots.* New York: Ballantine Books, 1991.

Williamson, Darcy, and Lisa Railsback. *Cooking with the Spirit: North American Indian Food and Fact.* Bend, Ore.: Maverick, 1988.

Winch, Terence, and Cheryl Wilson, eds. *All Roads Are Good: Native Voices on Life and Culture.* Washington, D.C.: National Museum of the American Indian, Smithsonian Institution, 1994.

Wolf, Linda, and the Editors of Time-Life Books. *The Cooking of the Caribbean Islands.* New York: Time-Life Books, 1970.

Permissions

≈ Detail from *The Exploits of Poor Wolf,* Hidatsa Second Chief, circa early 1900s. Artist unknown. (T4/2446A)

INDEX